THE
WONDER
OF

Birds

A Celebration of Birds

By Louis J. Halle

Although I would not want to live in a world without birds, I could not easily say why. It is the same with music. As I write these words, I have just come from a performance of Bach's *Christmas Oratorio*, in the religious setting of a cathedral, and am poignantly aware of how desolate life would be in a world without music.

I could say that birds and music are alike beautiful, and that I would not want to live in a world without beauty. But this would be to beg the question by answering it with a word that itself needs explaining.

Let us, by way of attempting a fuller answer, say that all of us inhabit two worlds at once, an ideal world of the mind and a day-to-day world in which all sorts of things are profoundly wrong. Reading my daily paper, I feel myself living in a world of disharmony, a world at war with itself, one in which people make desperate shift to meet dangers and horrors that bear in on them from all sides. I have the impression of a world that has lost its way. Then, however, I go to the cathedral where they are performing the *Oratorio*, and it is as if I had emerged from the darkness into light, from falsehood into truth.

I find in birds and nature, quite literally, what I find in music. There is, for example, rhythm, and there are rhythms within rhythms. One rhythm is that of the four seasons, marked by all birds because the lives of all move in seasonal cycles—the cycles of migration, of courtship and nesting, of shedding and renewing plumage, the cycle of silence and song. Even in the flight of birds there are rhythms within rhythms.

Wood Thrushes fight for water during a dry spell. By John Trott.

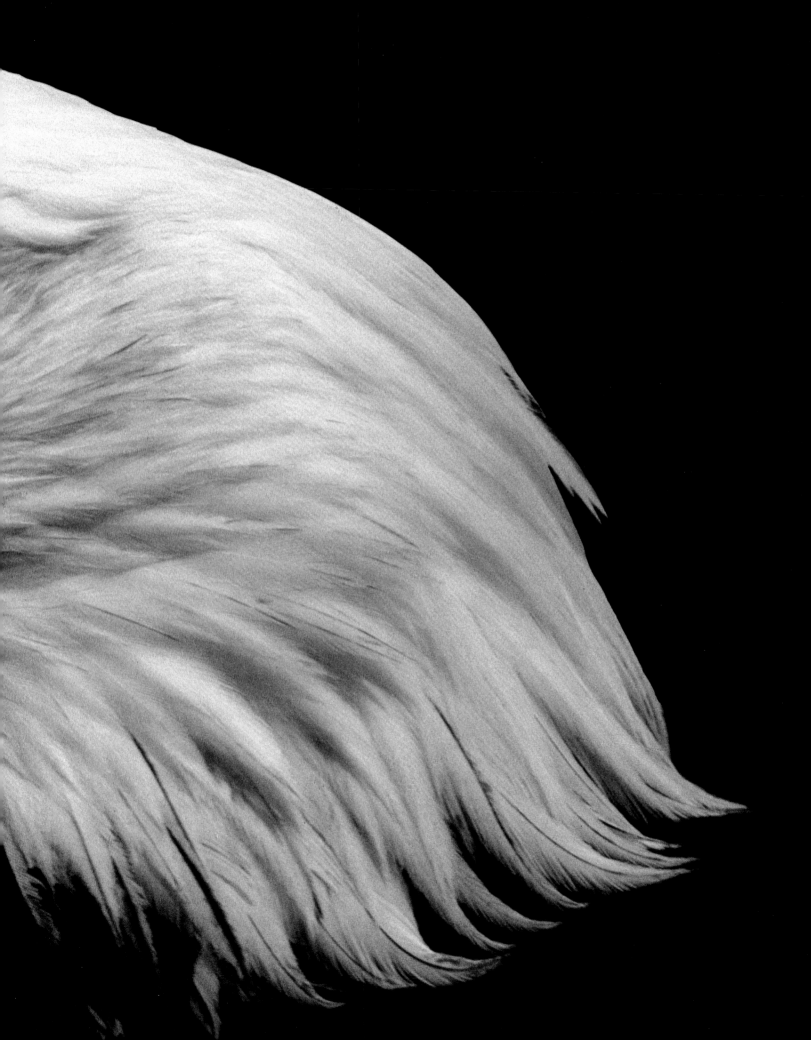

Every morning before breakfast, in the Swiss city of Geneva where I live, I walk down one bank of the river that divides it and up the other, crossing and recrossing its bridges. Although in winter it is still full night when I leave home, the small and graceful Black-headed Gulls are already on the move, anticipating the dawn. Lighted from below by the streetlamps, they form a river of birds over the river of water, flowing in undulations on their way to feeding grounds downstream. (In the evening, conforming to a circadian rhythm, they fly upstream again to their nocturnal roosts.) There is one rhythm in their wingbeats, a longer one in their collective undulations. As dawn comes, against the ever lightening sky, black clouds of starlings also enter, as counterpoint, into the harmony of a new day. Bands of wild ducks, high up, are also, like the gulls, on their way downriver—one band, and then another, and then another. All this is an overture, repeated daily, but changing with the seasons, and so part of an annual rhythm as well. I associate it with Bach's *Oratorio* rather than with what, when the magic of the birds' dawn is over, I shall be reading in the newspaper.

At the end of winter the songbirds start to sing, and each song has its own characteristic rhythm. This is literally music. So is the hooting of Barred Owls at night.

For those of us who are, by temperament, perfectionists, birds represent a perfection not to be found in the world of the newspaper. The species of birds in the wider world of nature—more than 9,000, varying from hummingbirds to albatrosses, from wrens to peacocks— each represents a sort of completed perfection brought about through natural selection over more than a hundred million years since the crude and clumsy ancestral *Archaeopteryx*. What the German entomologist in Conrad's *Lord Jim* said of a butterfly might be said of any wood warbler, of a kestrel, or of a Green-winged Teal: "Look! The beauty—but that is nothing—look at the accuracy, the harmony. And so fragile! And so strong! And so exact! This is Nature—the balance of colossal forces. Every star is so—and every blade of grass stands *so*—and the mighty Kosmos in perfect equilibrium produces—this. This wonder; this masterpiece of Nature—the great artist."

This is what we mean by "beauty." It is the exemplification of a sublime order as opposed to the chaos of daily living in which we find ourselves immersed.

The world that birds represent has an amplitude in time and in space that the world of our daily preoccupations lacks. Any of us, translated from the present to a million years ago, would find no cities, no factories, no highways for trucks. He would find no bureaucracies processing paper in the compartmentalized layers of great office buildings. He would find no manuals setting forth Standard Operating Procedure for the destruction of cities on the other side of the world. But he would find swallows engaged in annual migrations between hemispheres; he would find thrushes scratching the ground with their feet under forest trees, overturning dead leaves with flicks of their bills; he would find seabirds wheeling over the open sea.

Not knowing what it may eventually lead to, I do not denigrate our half-formed civilization. For the present, however, it appears to be as precariously established on the surface of the earth as a house of cards. No wonder if we feel the need to apprehend, beneath the chaos it represents, the enduring natural order that is most vividly represented by the birds.

Most vividly represented by the birds—in part because they are the most visible among the higher forms of life. The mammals, over most of the world, are generally elusive or hidden: They creep through the grass, they hide in holes, or they come out only at night. But the birds are everywhere, displaying themselves as if in some public pageant. I cannot think, however, that the ubiquity and the relative visibility of birds suffice to explain their unique appeal. There is the power of flight that implies the open air and space—in the swallow as in the eagle. To those of us who are restive under the confinements of civilization, the freedom of a bird in the sky suggests the heaven of our dreams. No wonder that the angels of religious tradition, otherwise shaped like us mortals, have been given the singular addition of wings!

There is not only the beauty but its infinite variety. The beauty of the Hooded Warbler is one thing, that of the Black Tern another—that of the Golden Eagle, tilting this way and that on outstretched wings, still another. . . . (Let the reader extend this list, in his mind, to cover 9,000 species.) How perfectly each has become adapted over millions of years, by "the balance of colossal forces," to its own particular place in the wide world of nature!

The danger today is that this world of endlessly varied beauty, which has taken so long to evolve, will be smothered and extinguished by our expanding, if precarious, civilization. Therefore our most immediate practical concern must be to stop this from happening, to save what we can—as in a burning ship.

We shall not, however, save what we do not appreciate. It is the more shame, then, that so many of us, living in this world of birds, see them only with unseeing eyes. For all of us are surrounded by birds as by people.

Even for city dwellers, the observation of birds need not be confined to special occasions that entail excursions into the country. The adaptability of many species is such that they may come to abound in the metropolis, often more abundantly than in the countryside. At the height of the migration in spring or fall, there may be greater concentrations of warblers in New York's Central Park than in any comparable area outside the city. Before they were almost extirpated over most of the United States by our reckless dissemination of deadly pesticides, one frequently saw Bald Eagles within the city limits of Washington, D. C., hunting over bodies of water adjacent to the Potomac River. And I have seen a Golden Eagle pass high over the heart of Geneva. In the days before the pesticides, and perhaps again in days

to come, one might watch Peregrine Falcons hunting pigeons before the public library on New York's Fifth Avenue. Once I saw a Snowy Owl, on visit from the wastes of the Arctic, roosting on the ledge of a government building in the heart of Washington.

Those beautiful saw-toothed ducks, the Common Mergansers (called Goosanders in Europe), have taken to nesting in the Swiss city of Neuchâtel. Once in early spring I watched a female searching for a nesting site on rooftops in the very center of Geneva, even landing on a roof for the inspection of a chimney with a hollow that might have served in place of the usual hollow tree. Wild ducks on both sides of the Atlantic have discovered that, in the hunting season, they are safe only on urban waters. In Scotland the kittiwakes, seabirds that spend most of the year far from land, have taken to building their nests on the windowsills of factory buildings, making them do for the ledges of cliffs. And some species of gulls have become city birds, raising their young on the flat roofs of city buildings.

Even now as I write, I look out of my window over the rooftops of a city where swifts and swallows describe arabesques in the air; where crows, each proceeding in direct line with steady wingbeat, cross one another's tracks; where cock pigeons on the ledges display before their mates; where a little falcon makes an unexpected appearance on swift wings, arousing a momentary alarm among the congregating sparrows in the gutters. (As soon as the falcon leaves, a thrush rises to a chimney pot, where he restores serenity by such song as no violinist ever surpassed.) It is wrong to regard all this as commonplace simply because it is common.

What I have just described is daily fare. But there are also the visitations of rare birds, which may occur anywhere at any time. Last winter an Arctic Loon, come from the far north, made itself at home by the river's embankment in the crowded center of Geneva.

But hurried pedestrians, passing just above, never saw it. Not far away, that daintiest of seabirds, a Red Phalarope, bobbed upon our urban waters, riding high like a cork, dipping and dabbling with its bill. Or it walked along the embankment, darting its bill at stone and cement, seeming as regardless of the pedestrians who loomed over it as they of it.

The greatest shame, however, is not so much our indifference to exotics as to the common birds that animate the skies almost everywhere. One of the frequent and wonderful sights over most of North America is that of the Red-winged Blackbirds in their joint aerial evolutions. A dense flock drifts this way and that against a sunset sky, like a piece of black chiffon turning and returning, twisting and untwisting. But to most of us it might as well be smoke.

There are those among us who will watch with fascination a television show on the birds of the Amazon, but not spare a glance for equally remarkable birds outside the window.

I say I would not want to live in a world without birds—and I say it with the more feeling because I have had the experience, having traveled to the only birdless region of continental extent in the world. On the ice in the middle of Antarctica, I found myself surrounded by an utter emptiness of life, except for the temporary intrusion of my fellow men. When, after four days, the airplane that was flying me out coasted down for a landing at the sea-washed edge of the continent, I saw below me several skuas in flight about a human encampment, whereupon my heart leaped in recognition. It was like seeing one's beloved again after the desolation of absence. Then I knew, as never before, how empty life would be in a world without birds.

The fact that appreciation comes first, if only because our kind will not conserve what it does not appreciate, is in itself all the justification needed for the volume these paragraphs introduce. Its implicit message is that, in the observation of birds, identification is not enough. Certainly there is no harm in the vast proliferation, over the past decades, of those who confine themselves to bird listing as a sport—which is to say, those who play the game of seeing how many species they can "get" in a day, or how large a life list they can build up. But there is something disturbing about the lister who, because he already has "got" the American Swallow-tailed Kite, will not spare even a glance for the beauty of its evolutions in the sky.

Granted that identification is the first requirement in the observation of a bird. But, just as there is more to a man than his outward appearance as one sees him walking down the street, so there is more to a bird than the feathered bundle one glimpses. There is its whole way of life the year around. To appreciate the Northern Parula (formerly called the Parula Warbler), one must know the family of wood warblers to which it belongs, a family like no other on earth, a family with its own unique beauty. One should have in mind its migration to wintering grounds in the American tropics, and its status as a harbinger of spring in the southern states. One should be familiar with the "quaint, drowsy, little gurgling sizzle" of its song—presented to my own mind's ear by a book before ever I heard it in actuality. These, and a thousand other features of its basic being, are none of them evident in the glimpse of a speck in the treetops. So one has to depend on books.

It is to meet this need with respect to North American birds that this book was designed. Here the annual rhythms and the daily rhythms that govern the lives of birds are set forth. Here are accounts of how birds fit their various environments. Here are accounts of their ancestry and of their relationships. Here are accounts of peculiarities in their behavior. Here we find cranes courting mates in spring and loons raising young in summer. Here we follow warblers south under an autumn sky, and wander with owls as they search for food in winter.

All this, which in its totality constitutes an account of beauty, is a joy to read in itself, as the illustrations are a joy to behold. For the real thing, however, we have to go out into the field. The basic service that this book performs is to equip us beforehand with the knowledge we need for the appreciation of what we will then see.

The Diversity of Birdlife

By Roger F. Pasquier

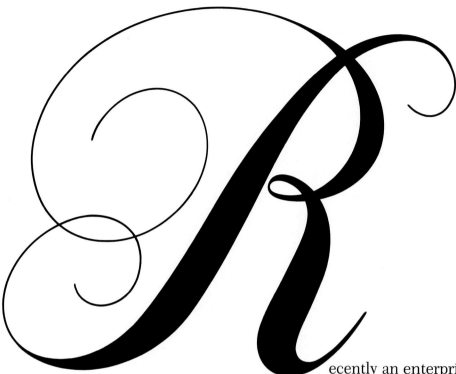

ecently an enterprising bird watcher gave himself the goal of seeing 700 species in North America in a single year. He had spent the prior year planning his route to cover every region and habitat of the continent, allowing extra time to dash from north to south or east to west whenever a particular rarity was reported. With much hard work and the help of local experts, he scored 699 by December 31. That we can even aspire to such a goal indicates that North America holds plenty of birds for all to see, even if we stay close to home. Indeed, much of the year so many North American species are on the move that we need not travel to them because they are traveling to us.

Approximately 650 species of birds regularly breed in North America. Some confine themselves to narrow ranges at the edges of the continent, in southern Florida, along the Mexican border, or in the far reaches of northwestern Alaska. Others are familiar sights the length and breadth of the land. In addition, birds from Europe, Asia, Central America, the Caribbean islands, and even Australia and New Zealand visit our shores. Some are annual migrants; others show up regularly as wanderers blown off course. A few are known from only a single sighting.

The birds that make their home in North America are a colorful and diverse assemblage. They range in size from tiny hummingbirds, wrens, and kinglets, only three or four inches long, to the four-foot-tall Whooping Crane. Some birds, like the male Painted Bunting, display the rainbow's most brilliant colors; others are elegant in black and white—

Pileated Woodpeckers feed their young. By Laura Riley.

18

Painting by John Gurche

or cryptic in mottled browns. Marvelous adaptations and extraordinary differences in behavior enable birds to thrive in almost every habitat.

Our birds range from permanent residents, which may spend their entire lives within a square mile, to long-distance migrants, a few of which travel 15,000 to 20,000 miles annually. If you live anywhere between Toronto and Corpus Christi, you can look forward each year to seeing birds from the northern forests and tundra traveling to the southern end of the hemisphere to escape winter entirely. If the winter north of you is unusually severe, food shortages might push unfamiliar species into your area. Spring and summer bring birds that spend at least half the year in the tropics and come north only to mate and raise young. After their brief time here, they quickly return to the south.

Migrations take place nearly every month. From California to New England the first avian signs of spring often come in February. Other birds will not be heading north until early June. By the Fourth of July the first shorebirds are on our beaches, bound for their winter homes in South America, and waterfowl are still traveling south at Christmas.

Across the continent millions of birds take part in the breathtaking spectacle of migration—ducks and geese along the coasts and rivers; hawks on the ridges; warblers, orioles, tanagers in the woodlands; sparrows in the fields. This combination of migrants is uniquely American and, for diversity, equaled in few other parts of the world.

Migration, nesting, molt, and other seasonal activities take place at the same time year after year, generation after generation. What keeps the birds on such a predictable course? As in humans, much behavior is controlled by a few glands that secrete hormones into the bloodstream. Ornithologists are still investigating the complex functions of these glands, probably stimulated by changes in day length, which activate impulses to migrate, breed, and molt. The pituitary gland affects the instinct to incubate eggs; the thyroid gland controls sexual development and molt. The parathyroid glands regulate the amount of calcium in the bloodstream and thus affect eggshell formation. The adrenal glands raise the level of sugar in the blood for sudden bursts of energy.

As the most highly visible group of wild animals around us, birds provide excellent opportunities to study aspects of behavior and evolution difficult to see in the shier mammals and the scarcer amphibians and reptiles. How have birds adapted to exploit so many different types of habitat? Do birds compete with one another? Why do birds sing more in spring than in other seasons? How do the migrants find their way on their long annual trips? Can birds survive the changes humans are making to the world? All these and other questions can be answered, at least in part, by careful observation of the birds around us.

People have been watching birds since long before the invention of the field guide and binoculars. The first humans surely observed birds in order to catch and eat them and, later, to tame them. Birds must also have been revered by the primitive people who depicted them on cave walls in France and Spain as early as 16,000 B.C. Ancient Sumerians and Egyptians decorated their residences, temples, and tombs with paintings of birds. Several of these are recognizable species of waterfowl still found in the region. The ancient Maya and Aztecs of the New World carved birds of wood and stone. The Resplendent Quetzal, with its long green plumes, embodied Quetzalcóatl, one of their major gods.

Aristotle (384-322 B.C.) was the first person we know of who looked at birds scientifically. He described the physiology, reproduction, and ecology of what he considered to be 170 species. A few other Greeks and Romans made similar observations, but for many centuries thereafter most bird lore was more fanciful.

Ideas about migration reveal how scientific observation has improved through time. Although Aristotle wrote of the migration of cranes and pelicans, he thought swallows retired to mountain peaks in the fall, shed their feathers, and hibernated until spring. Until the 16th century no one doubted that swallows hibernated, although many authorities believed they slept through the winter in the muddy bottoms of lakes rather than on mountaintops. In 1703 an anonymous essay published in England asserted that swallows flew to the moon to hibernate; the trip took 60 days. Not until travelers began exploring the African tropics—and seeing familiar European birds there in winter—were people persuaded that birds flew south to escape the effects of cold weather.

From Africa and the New World, explorers sent thousands of bird specimens, dead or alive, to the European capitals of science. It rapidly became evident that there were far more bird species in the world than the early classifiers had imagined. In the mid-18th century the scientist Carl von Linné devised a classification system that helped make sense of the chaos of information about the natural world. Linné, a Swede better known by his latinized name Linnaeus, assigned each plant and animal a unique two-word name based on Latin. (The first word is the genus, a group of closely related species; the second word refers to the species.) Because no two species have the same combination of names, the Linnaean system distinguished each species from all the others and showed which ones were most closely related. This system, a great accomplishment of 18th-century science, enabled scientists to integrate newly discovered birds into the framework of families and species already known. We still use this system of classification.

During the 18th and 19th centuries the primary task of ornithologists and naturalists was to describe all the "new" birds from around the world, to determine their ranges, and to assign their place in the Linnaean order. The educated public, also interested in these discoveries, encouraged the publication of lavish books with color plates. In response to this demand John James Audubon produced *The Birds of America,* a series of 435 life-size, hand-colored engravings of every North American bird he had observed or received as a specimen.

The 20th century has witnessed the greatest progress in bird study, mainly in the fields of behavior, ecology, evolution, and migration. Today scientists use advanced equipment to assist their research. Migrant birds are followed by radar, tracked with tiny radio transmitters, and observed in planetariums with different patterns of stars in tests of how birds navigate. We can answer many questions, but ornithologists are still debating basic issues like the origin of birds. (Continued on page 30)

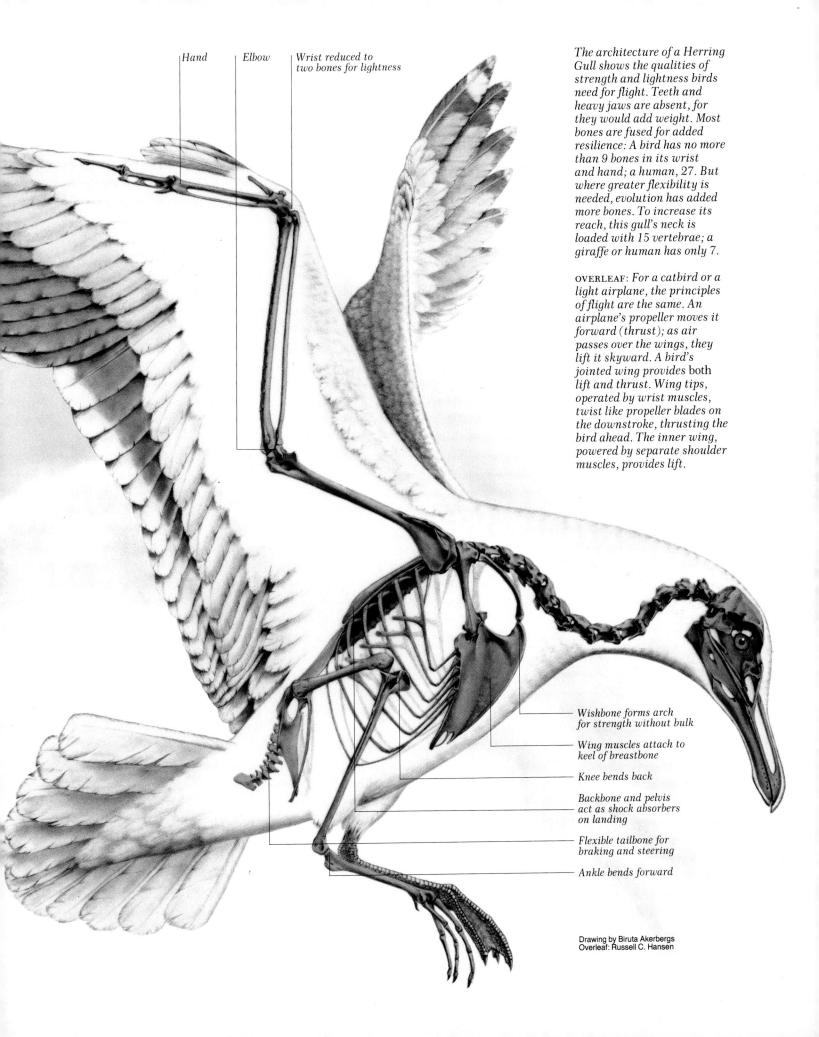

Hand   Elbow   Wrist reduced to
two bones for lightness

The architecture of a Herring Gull shows the qualities of strength and lightness birds need for flight. Teeth and heavy jaws are absent, for they would add weight. Most bones are fused for added resilience: A bird has no more than 9 bones in its wrist and hand; a human, 27. But where greater flexibility is needed, evolution has added more bones. To increase its reach, this gull's neck is loaded with 15 vertebrae; a giraffe or human has only 7.

OVERLEAF: *For a catbird or a light airplane, the principles of flight are the same. An airplane's propeller moves it forward (thrust); as air passes over the wings, they lift it skyward. A bird's jointed wing provides both lift and thrust. Wing tips, operated by wrist muscles, twist like propeller blades on the downstroke, thrusting the bird ahead. The inner wing, powered by separate shoulder muscles, provides lift.*

Wishbone forms arch for strength without bulk

Wing muscles attach to keel of breastbone

Knee bends back

Backbone and pelvis act as shock absorbers on landing

Flexible tailbone for braking and steering

Ankle bends forward

Drawing by Biruta Akerbergs
Overleaf: Russell C. Hansen

Like a seaplane, a web-footed Greater Shearwater (left) gathers speed until it has enough lift for takeoff. On long slender wings designed for gliding, not flapping, shearwaters skim over the waves and frigatebirds soar for hours without a wingbeat. This Magnificent Frigatebird (below) puffs up his scarlet throat sac to attract a mate.

OVERLEAF: On broad steady wings a Bald Eagle can cruise lazily on a level course or spiral slowly upward on a thermal—a column of air rising from the sun-warmed earth. Slotted wing feathers steady soaring birds and let them maneuver in shifting air currents. Fanlike tails steer these majestic aerialists and add to their sail surface.

Farrell Grehan. Left: William Ervin. Overleaf: Glenn W. Elison

The oldest bird we know of, *Archaeopteryx* ("ancient wing"), lived when the biggest of the dinosaurs roamed the earth about 140 million years ago. Although it may have inhabited other parts of the world, its bones have been found in only one region of southern Germany. Without the clear impressions of feathers in the fine-grained limestone, *Archaeopteryx* could easily have passed for a two-legged reptile. Unlike modern birds, *Archaeopteryx* had toothed jaws, a head covered with scales, well-developed claws on its wings, and a bony tail. It was unquestionably a bird, but to what extent could it fly? Since all modern birds that fly have asymmetrical flight feathers like those of *Archaeopteryx*, it is logical to believe that it too could fly. But this ancient creature may have been limited to gliding flight.

Why did feathers evolve in the first place? One theory proposes that the reptile ancestors of birds were already warm blooded and the first feathers insulated their bodies from cold. Another theory suggests that feathers originated as elongated scales that helped shade the body from intense heat. According to both theories, flight came later. Neither, however, accounts for the complex structure of feathers that makes them so well suited for flying. Another theory may come closer to the answer. If the ancestors of birds lived in trees and jumped from branch to branch, then the slightest elongation of a reptilian scale on the front of the arm would aid in parachuting or jumping. The ability to fly would grow as these elongated scales, or rudimentary feathers, developed.

We do not know whether *Archaeopteryx* was the direct ancestor of any modern birds, but this crow-size creature probably lived in a world that included other birds of about the same size or smaller. Nevertheless, nearly all the early fossils we have are of large, flightless water birds found in 120-million-year-old chalk beds in western Kansas, once an inland sea. *Hesperornis* ("western bird"), a toothed, loonlike swimmer, may have given birth to live young and never come to dry land. Its wings, no more than stubs, were useless for flight. *Ichthyornis* ("fish bird"), the first known bird with wings developed for sustained flight, was the size of a gull, had teeth, and probably ate fish.

As the epochs succeeded one another, climates and landforms changed, and new birds evolved. Many familiar families appeared about 60 million years ago: herons, ducks, vultures, hawks, grouse, cranes, owls. Songbirds, the most recent group to make their debut, emerged about 30 million years ago. Favored by flight and with little competition from earthbound creatures, the ancestors of many of the species we see today multiplied. Other birds, like vultures with wings stretching 12 feet from tip to tip, disappeared during the ice ages.

What a pity some of the birds that thrived only a few thousand years ago were not spared! New fossil discoveries continually reveal fascinating species. In 1980 scientists unearthed a predator that had soared over Argentina between 5 and 8 million years ago. (*Continued on page 38*)

For survival's sake, not vanity's, birds must clean and oil their feathers regularly. With its ponderous bill a young Brown Pelican (below) in Florida's famed Everglades squeezes oil from the preen gland near its tail, then anoints each feather. Oil keeps feathers waterproof, supple, and in good shape. Gracing a South Carolina cypress swamp, a Great Egret and its snowy white brood (opposite) settle in for an afternoon of preening and resting. With its beak the adult combs its aigrettes, the filmy finery of mating season worn like a nuptial veil.

Jeff Foott. Opposite: David S. Soliday

Wings to the wind, a preening Anhinga displays a badge of its species—silvery wing patches. The wind and sun dry its sodden feathers, which become waterlogged when this agile swimmer and diver pursues underwater prey. Like grebes, the heavy-boned Anhinga sinks in the water by squeezing air out of its plumage and the air sacs that make its body float. The half-submerged bird prowls southern waters with only its small head and long, sinuous neck visible (upper). This up-periscope position has given the Anhinga a nickname—the snakebird. With its stiletto bill this master harpooner skewers fish, water snakes, and even baby alligators. But the dinner may become the diner when a full-grown alligator, perhaps sensing a quick meal, stalks a resting Anhinga (center). Wings drenched from a recent dive, the bird would have trouble flying—and so flees to shore (lower). The alligator cruises away in search of easier prey.

Art Wolfe. Opposite: Rachel Cobb

J. H. Robinson (also below)

Why do birds of the same species sometimes look so different? A genetic mutation can produce a crow, usually black from bill to tail, that is snowy white (right). Albino birds lack the pigment that gives them color; this loss of camouflage makes them easy targets for predators. And because albinos look so different, they are often harassed by normal members of their species. Age accounts for the contrast between two White Ibis (upper). A mottled juvenile must wait more than two years before it acquires its white adult plumage. Depending on their genetic makeup, screech-owls (lower) may be mostly gray or red. Such inherited color is not influenced by age or sex.

M. P. Kahl. Right: Karl H. Maslowski

Ron Austing

36

The largest flying bird known, it weighed about 200 pounds and could have looked a 6-foot-tall person in the eye. About the size of a modern hang glider, it shadowed the landscape on wings spanning 25 feet. The largest flying bird today, the Wandering Albatross, glides over the far southern oceans on wings that stretch 11.5 feet. The North American bird with the greatest wingspan—9.5 feet—is the California Condor.

Today no one would have difficulty distinguishing birds from other members of the animal kingdom. Plato described man as a creature with two legs and no feathers; we could describe birds as creatures with two legs *and* feathers. All birds have feathers. All have toes covered with scales, revealing their reptilian ancestry. All have toothless bills with varied shapes that indicate a host of feeding adaptations. All are keenly sighted, especially the birds of prey. All lay eggs. Most birds fly, but there are numerous exceptions, including the Ostrich, kiwis, and rheas. There are also flightless ducks and parrots, to name two families better known for their swift fliers. Penguins literally "fly" underwater, pumping their flipperlike wings and using their webbed feet as rudders.

Feathers, the most distinctive feature of birds, come in several forms: smooth ones to cover the body, fluffy ones beneath these to keep the body warm, and long, stiff feathers for support in flight. Several thousand feathers cloak the average bird. A Ruby-throated Hummingbird has more than 1,500, an Eastern Meadowlark about 4,600. Waterfowl often have the greatest number of feathers in proportion to their size because they need heavy insulation. A Mallard is covered with 12,000 feathers, while a Bald Eagle, several times larger, has only 7,100. Of the 25,216 feathers plucked from a Tundra Swan (formerly known as the Whistling Swan), 80 percent came from its head and long neck, which are submerged as it feeds on aquatic plants.

If you look carefully at a large feather from a bird's wing, you will notice that the central shaft is spongy, making the feather lighter and better adapted for flying. Slender branches, or barbs, slant diagonally from either side of the shaft. You can easily pull the barbs apart and then, by pressing above and below the separation, zip them together the way a bird would preen with its bill. From each side of the barb grow hundreds of smaller side branches, or barbules, that overlap in a herringbone pattern. Minute hooks on the barbules lock the branches together and make feathers sleek and supple yet stiff enough for flying or swimming. One barb on a crane's feather has about 1,200 barbules, which means the entire feather has well over a million barbules.

Feathers, together with adaptations of muscles, heart, bones, and lungs, make birds the most efficient of flying machines. Feathers have many advantages. They are light. They are regularly replaced when worn, lost, or damaged. Each is individually attached to a muscle for greater maneuverability. Feathers enable birds to ride effortlessly on the wind, to travel faster than 100 miles per hour, to hover and fly backwards, to fly more than 48 hours without resting, and to migrate thousands of miles a year. No bird does all of these things, but feathers make them all possible. Swifts, for example, are such accomplished aerialists that they feed, drink, bathe, court, and even mate while flying. In addition to flying at the great speeds (80 miles per hour and faster) that have given them their name, swifts sometimes spend the night on the wing a few thousand feet above the ground.

The shape of the wings and tail tells us at a glance how specialized a bird is for flight. Some of the fastest fliers—falcons and swallows, for example—have long pointed wings and long narrow tails. This streamlined profile creates the least resistance as the bird moves through the air. The Peregrine Falcon, diving after prey, has been clocked at 175 miles per hour. The broader wings and tail of slower fliers, such as vultures, eagles, and storks, catch every movement of air so these birds can soar and wheel high in the sky. Birds such as pheasants and grouse, which seldom fly, have short rounded wings that provide quick lift but little sustaining power. Their leg muscles are much more developed than those used in flight. Because the hardest working muscles are nourished by more capillaries and are therefore darker, earthbound birds like chickens and turkeys have "dark meat" in their legs and "white meat" in their breasts. In most birds the breast muscles form the dark meat.

The bird's skeleton, a marvel of flight engineering, fuses lightness with strength. Most birds do not have a bone like the one in humans that separates the nasal cavity from the mouth—one of the many adaptations that keep flying weight to a minimum. Their skulls are usually paper thin. The heads of woodpeckers, however, are specially reinforced to absorb the constant stress of hammering trees. Many powerful fliers are equipped with hollow bones, which are filled with air sacs to increase buoyancy. The skeleton of the frigatebird, a soarer with a seven-foot wingspan, weighs only four ounces—less than its feathers. Hollow bones are stronger than solid bones of the same weight because they bend more easily and the air inside them absorbs shocks. Longer wing bones are reinforced with struts, a device also found in airplanes.

Strong fliers have proportionately larger hearts that pump blood more rapidly than those of nonfliers, weak fliers, and soaring birds. When hovering, a hummingbird beats its wings about 50 times a second, with its heart pulsing 1,200 times a minute. The lungs, aided by air sacs in the bones and other cavities—even the toes—supply the oxygen needed for flight. The reproductive system also enhances aerodynamic efficiency: The testes of male birds expand in size and weight only during the brief season they are producing sperm.

While the most important function of feathers is to work in concert with all the internal adaptations for flight, they serve other purposes as well. You can often predict a bird's habitat by the color of its plumage. Streaked brown birds like sparrows or grouse usually dwell on the ground. Woodpeckers and other small black-and-white birds cling to tree trunks. Green birds live in the foliage. Even the bold orange-and-black pattern of the male Northern Oriole may make it seem to disappear in the flickering light of the treetops.

Attracted by running water, a Summer Tanager dunks in a small Texas pool. Bathing keeps plumage clean and tidy and in good condition. Some birds bathe by fluttering through raindrops or rolling in snow. Swifts and swallows fly low over ponds for a quick dip; warblers flit among wet leaves; larks lie belly down and spread their wings in the rain; hummingbirds shower under lawn sprinklers.

OVERLEAF: *Two bathing beauties, an Indigo Bunting and a Summer Tanager, flick wings and tails to splash water over their backs. After bathing, birds usually fly to a nearby perch to groom and dry their feathers.*

Opposite and overleaf: Barth Schorre

Whether camouflaging or not, colors and patterns also help birds communicate. A male Red-winged Blackbird displays his red-and-yellow shoulder patches to inform others that he occupies a territory. Closely related male ducks like the Mallard and the Northern Pintail have strikingly different plumages, which help the females identify the correct mate. The female ducks usually wear browns or grays, streaked or spotted to blend with the nesting grounds, where they bear the major burden of incubating eggs and raising young.

The colors of feathers sometimes play other roles. Black pigment in the wing tips of many large white birds, such as Whooping Cranes and Snow Geese, makes the ends of the feathers more resistant to wear. Lack of pigment in the wings and tails of albinos makes their feathers brittle and may reduce their ability to fly. The buff color of many desert birds helps insulate them from the strong light and extreme temperatures.

Ornithologists group the world's 9,000 or so bird species in about 170 families. Some families contain only a single species—the Ostrich, for example; others have a few hundred—hawks, pigeons, parrots, sparrows. Birds are not, of course, distributed evenly over the globe. Some families, such as gulls, hawks, owls, pigeons, swifts, and swallows, are found throughout the world, while others inhabit only one continent. Certain species are confined to a single region: The Seaside Sparrow lives only in salt marshes along the Atlantic and Gulf coasts of the United States.

Where did the birds of North America originate? Europe and Asia have given us titmice, larks, and many other songbirds. Our pigeons and kingfishers may have come from Australia and New Guinea by way of Eurasia. The hummingbirds, flycatchers, and tanagers that spend their summers in North America originated in the rain forests of tropical America. Many of "our" migratory species actually spend more time in the tropics than they do here.

Several bird families originated in North America. Most of these, such as mockingbirds, vireos, and wood warblers, have expanded into the American tropics, while a few, like grouse, have filtered into Europe and Asia. The wren family, now widespread throughout the New World, has one species that has spread across northern Eurasia—the Winter Wren.

A distinct community of birds lives in each of North America's five major habitats: the treeless tundra of the far north; the coniferous forests south of the tundra, stretching from northern New England across Canada to Alaska; the deciduous forests of the eastern United States; the grasslands of central North America; and the deserts in the southwest. Bird watchers know that within these habitats many subtle factors— vegetation, water, soil, altitude, temperature—determine where certain birds will be found. One of the most rewarding experiences of watching birds is learning the ways they partition their environment to avoid competition and to exploit a particular niche. Observing a few birds in any habitat will give you the knack. (*Continued on page 48*)

Bates Littlehales, National Geographic Photographer

44

Birds bathe year round—but not always in water. Basking in the sun releases vitamin D from oil in the Blue Jay's feathers. Absorbed through the skin or swallowed during preening, vitamin D may prevent rickets. Heat may also cause pests to migrate from the body to the head, where they can be scratched. Like a person with an itch, this American Avocet (upper) scratches for relief and also to spread preen oil on its head. Gambel's Quail (lower) and other desert dwellers dry-clean themselves with dust to soak up excess oil and control parasites. To discourage such lodgers, some birds rub their plumage with acid-producing ants or anything that burns, even lighted cigarettes.

Jim Brandenburg

Stephen J. Krasemann, DRK Photo

A flock of dowitchers and Surfbirds dozes in the warm afternoon sun on the Copper River in Alaska (below). Shorebirds spend many daylight hours resting on open beaches or mud flats, where they can easily see predators approaching. Most birds sleep with their heads resting on their backs and their bills tucked securely under the shoulder feathers—a posture that gives them warm air to breathe and protects their eyes and faces from the cold. Although it is not known why, even birds in warm climates, like the flamingo (opposite), sleep this way. The seven-pound flamingo sleeps standing on one leg. Shorebirds do the same to conserve precious body heat that may otherwise be lost through their unfeathered legs. Perching birds sometimes sleep on one leg. Special muscles and tendons automatically lock the toes around the branch when the bird lands on it and the leg bends. This allows the bird to perch securely when awake and to sleep peacefully without falling off.

Jonathan Blair. Opposite: Jim Brandenburg

From an ocean beach you may see gulls, terns, and cormorants flying over the water. The gulls, with relatively broad wings, ride the wind and then swoop to the water to pick a fish or squid from the surface. The smaller and more streamlined terns, with narrower wings less useful for soaring, hover when they spot a fish a few inches below the surface and then plunge into the water. The lumbering cormorants often rest on the water and then swim several feet below in search of fish.

On the beach, gulls scavenge for animal matter that has washed up; a few fly off with clams and drop them on the ground to break. Some gulls have learned to drop shellfish on roadways and tennis courts. Sanderlings run along the edge of the retreating waves, searching for tiny mollusks. Red Knots, sandpipers larger than the Sanderling, pluck bigger shellfish from the surface of the wet sand, while dowitchers use their long bills to probe underneath, jabbing their heads up and down like sewing machine needles. Ruddy Turnstones pry under pebbles to find food. Oystercatchers take the meat out of clams and other bivalves by inserting their long sturdy bills and popping open the shells.

In a woodland you may find several species flocking together. By forming a group, the birds have more eyes available to spot lurking predators, even though the group as a whole is more conspicuous than a solitary bird. Here, too, each bird is a specialist. A Hairy Woodpecker climbs a tree trunk, hammering with its chisel-like bill for insects underneath the bark. Stiff tail feathers help prop the bird when climbing or resting. A nuthatch moves headfirst down the trunk as easily as up, using its stout bill to probe bark crevices for insect eggs or pupae. The smaller Brown Creeper climbs up the trunk in circles, reaching in narrow cracks with its fine, slightly curved bill. Chickadees flit through the branches, often hanging upside down to pick insects off the twigs. Kinglets flutter up to the leaves and then hover to pluck insects.

At a pond or lake, Mallards tip their tails up and nibble succulent vegetation growing at the bottom. Canada Geese, much larger and with longer necks, can reach plants in deeper water. A Pied-billed Grebe sinks slowly in the water, then swims below in pursuit of tadpoles. Swallows skim the surface to pick up insects or dip into the water to bathe on the wing. A Belted Kingfisher perches on a branch at the edge of the water, waiting to spot a fish. On the shore a Green-backed Heron (formerly the Green Heron) watches for minnows, while a Great Blue Heron stands on longer legs in the deeper water, eyeing larger fish to spear with its rapier bill. In the reeds, Marsh Wrens and Swamp Sparrows search for seeds and insects. From the willows beyond the reeds, Willow Flycatchers dart out to catch insects.

Everywhere in North America, in all seasons, similar scenes can be enjoyed by anyone who will go out and look. Though you may not see 700 birds in a year or even in a lifetime, the rewards of learning more about birds and their place in the natural world can be yours every day.

To catch its dinner, the Green-backed Heron slowly extends its flexible neck and gently drops a pellet in the water (below). Eyes fixed on the bobbing bait, the bird keeps a low profile by crouching motionless until its quarry swims by. Then, lightning quick, the heron strikes (right)—and rarely misses. Sometimes it baits and snatches an unwary victim every minute for almost half an hour. The bird grips the fish with its two-inch bill (lower right), then flips it around and gulps it down headfirst.

50

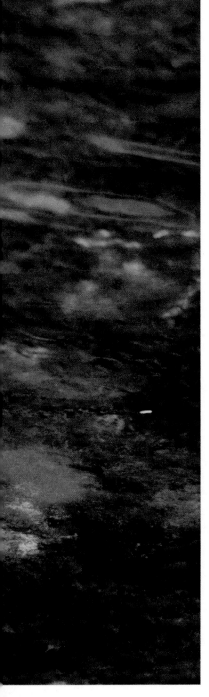

Feuding neighbors: A feisty mockingbird dive-bombs a caracara, then fans its wings to drive the falcon from mutual nesting grounds. The mockingbird defends its territory against all enemies —dogs, cats, snakes, and even its own image reflected in a car's hubcap. The tiny Rufous Hummingbird will dive fearlessly at blackbirds or chipmunks lurking near its nest, while Common Terns bomb intruders with foul-smelling dung and peck their heads. Comrades at arms, many species of small birds mob together to intimidate owls, hawks, and other foes. Flocking birds sometimes mass tightly in flight, making it difficult for hunters on the wing to single out a victim.

Gilbert Palmer (also opposite)

Return and Renewal

By Paul A. Johnsgard

he spring season comes reluctantly to the Great Plains. Along the Platte River of Nebraska in early March, the elms and cottonwoods etch their leafless silhouettes on a chill landscape, where prairie grasses lie brown and dormant. Beside the stream, pools of standing water put on icy roofs each night, reminders that winter could close in again at whim.

But for the watchful the first signs of renewal are there. The wind from the dark river carries with it the thin but certain smell of fecundity, a suggestion of the teeming microscopic life that thrives in the frigid stream. And in the soggy fields by the river's edge, the winter wheat is sprouting green from the black earth.

Then the Sandhill Cranes return and the coming of spring is no longer in doubt. Their voices rise from afar like the bugles of a distant regiment. It is difficult to pick out the rattling *garooo-a-a-a* of an individual bird, for the great mass lives and moves and calls as if it were a single organism composed of a hundred thousand working parts, awesome and seemingly unstoppable as it approaches. Thousands of the steely gray birds, with red crowns and six-foot wingspans, pour through the sky in undulating scrawls and patterns.

The sight alone is impressive, but it is the collective voice of the flock that lingers in one's memory. There is something wild and untouchable in it, something primeval that reaches back through the millennia to a spring when the cranes inhabited an earth unencumbered by humans. The cranes are a foretaste of the season, for like them, millions of birds

Male prairie chickens battle for mates. By Entheos.

will soon be on the move throughout North America. To the Ruby-throated Hummingbird, smaller than some moths, spring means a March or April flight of some 600 miles across the Gulf of Mexico from Yucatán, then a push northward into the eastern half of the continent to a familiar territory that holds the promise of mates and nectar-filled flowers. Half a globe away White-rumped Sandpipers are leaving their winter quarters in Tierra del Fuego, beginning an 8,000-mile journey that will end on the arctic tundra in June.

Other birds travel hardly any distance. Dark-eyed Juncos that wintered in the Virginia Piedmont simply fly 20 or 30 miles west, seeking higher elevations in the Appalachian Mountains. There they reunite with others that wintered in the Shenandoah Valley beyond the Blue Ridge Mountains, eastern rampart of the Appalachians.

For the 650 or so species of birds that breed in North America, the mandate of spring is the same: to replicate themselves. The wonder lies in the diversity of the process, the myriad ways in which our birds accomplish that mandate, often in spite of daunting obstacles. Each species has its own method of courtship and breeding, a ritualized strategy for survival so deeply imbued in the genes that no individual bird has to figure out how it ought to proceed.

For the Sandhill Cranes that visit Nebraska, the plan requires an arduous odyssey: first a flight from as far as northern Mexico or the Texas coast, then a long sweep north to arctic breeding grounds in Alaska, northern Canada, and, for some, even eastern Siberia. The cranes fly with the spring as it unrolls across the land, for spring means food, and food means fuel for their long journey. The Platte River Valley is their most crucial stopover.

By the time they reach the Platte, many of the mature cranes have already formed attachments, or pair bonds, one of the first steps in the breeding cycle of all birds. After the pair is formed, the two cranes will continue to court each other through a long process that ensures they will copulate with the proper sex and species at just the right time—when the female's eggs are ready and the male is primed to fertilize them. Most birds go through a similar cycle, in which the length varies from species to species—a few minutes to several months.

For now the paired cranes stay close to their partners when feeding in fields and meadows. Sometimes the two birds break into spontaneous dance, bouncing around like rubber balls, their wings partly spread to cushion their descent. Dancing cranes have been seen leaping as high as 12 feet. Facing each other, they may call in unison and occasionally bow as if in greeting, then toss sticks or grass into the air. The calling and dancing strengthen the bond between them.

Such monogamous partnerships are common among long-lived birds and last as long as both birds survive. But scientists do not fully understand why cranes pair for life. The demands of their breeding habitat offer at least a partial answer. Spring and summer on the tundra are rich but fleeting, and food for the nestlings is available for only a short time. By the time the cranes reach their nesting grounds, they have little leisure for lengthy courtship displays or for inspecting prospective mates. Thus the cranes keep the same partner, year in and year out, and extend their courtship over the long weeks of travel from winter to summer quarters.

But the world of birds is full of contradictions. Some species mate with as many partners as possible. And in others the customs vary with individuals. Faithfulness, or the lack of it, may depend in part on the abundance of food. If plenty is available and the female parent can gather enough to care for her young, the male may be less motivated to form a permanent arrangement with her than to search out other mates and thus spread his genes more widely.

So it is with hummingbirds. Working alone, the female begins to build her nest and may copulate with the first male that happens by. Then they part company, she to finish the nest and raise the brood, he to mate with other females. The male Yellow-headed Blackbird may father several families over the course of a season. He starts by mating with one female; only rarely does he help raise their young, which leave the nest in less than two weeks. Usually he searches for another partner and begins the cycle again. In other species the arrangements depend on local conditions. If a Red-winged Blackbird can attract only one female to his territory, he will have no choice but monogamy. If more are available, he will mate with two or three.

A limited sort of fidelity typifies most North American songbirds. They stay together through the mating season or until the young have left the nest. Then they separate. When spring returns, some of these birds renew their attachments with each other. Mockingbirds and cardinals have reunited with old mates in this way. But many scientists now believe that the birds are drawn to their former nesting territories, not to each other, and probably return each spring because they find safety and ample food there. They breed with last year's mate if he or she happens to be on the favored turf at the right moment.

Still, some mystery remains. Some species, such as the Lesser Goldfinch and the Cedar Waxwing, may form pairs *before* they reach their breeding grounds, as do the Sandhill Cranes. Their loyalty seems to be to each other. No one knows exactly why this is so; perhaps finding the right mate early contributes more to their breeding success than finding the right territory.

Such questions surround the courtship of birds. Why does one bird choose a particular mate over others? How does one advertise his or her availability? And how does one accept or reject explicit overtures? The answers are as varied as the immensity of birdlife.

For some species, song appears to serve as the inducement to copulation. Others depend primarily on visual signals, as ducks do. Still others use a combination of sight and sound; Sandhill Cranes are in this category. For them the urge to breed comes relatively late in life—at three, four, or five years of age. As the days grow longer in springtime, increased sunlight triggers the release of hormones in maturing males. And while the males gradually grow more aggressive, the females become less so; lulled by the estrogens now coursing through their bodies, the females become more tolerant, more receptive.

During their first year of life, both sexes lose the rust-tinged feathers of their youth and replace them with plumage of lustrous gray. Their crowns later become featherless crimson skullcaps, a badge of maturity. Reacting to such changes, parents no longer tolerate the presence of the youngsters they have guarded since hatching and led on their long migrations. Eventually the parents may even rush at their offspring and, in a burst of wing waving and raucous calling, shoo them away. Now the immature cranes are on their own—at least until the fall migration, when family bonds may again close the generation gap.

A long apprenticeship has helped the young birds learn the way before they take on the responsibilities of leading their own youngsters down the dangerous migratory corridors of North America. And it has given them ample time to practice their prolonged courtship rituals, full of complexity and subtlety.

Because all male and female cranes look alike, they must master a special "language" of courtship. Otherwise they might invest months or years developing a homosexual pair bond that would, of course, result in failure at breeding time. To avoid such confusion, each crane is fully programmed and predisposed for the rituals of its particular sex.

The male crane always takes the first step, not knowing whether his intended partner is male or female. He approaches the other crane as if he means to fight it. He may preen his back or belly feathers in a gesture of warning—the crane equivalent of a dog baring its teeth. He expands his red crown, which brightens as blood rushes into it. Then he waits. If the other crane is a male, there could be a fight. But if it is a female, she may retract her red crown and lower her head—and the measured course of courtship has begun. Over the months, or even years, before mating will take place, the pair continue this testing, the male advancing, the female retreating.

Once the cranes begin to tolerate each other, they reinforce their growing bond by responding as a unit to any threat—the approach of a human, for example. The female crane usually begins calling first, her voice clattering like machine-gun fire. In an instant her mate joins in, harmonizing and tossing his head up and down. The display, known as a unison call, is an unmistakable symbol of the cranes' pair bond.

In their early courtship there is little evidence of personal attachment between the cranes. But in time they come to recognize each other— much as humans do—by voice, behavior, and facial features.

After a while together, some birds may even appear, to human eyes, to show personal attachments. W. H. Hudson, an English naturalist, once told of two wild geese that walked south in migration several days after their companions had flown away. The female had a broken wing. Every few minutes the male would fly ahead a few hundred yards, screaming. When she failed to fly with him, he would circle back and land 40 or 50 yards ahead of her. Thus they trudged on together, she unable to fly, he unwilling to abandon her. "In that sad anxious way," wrote Hudson, "they would journey on to the inevitable end" when she would almost surely fall to a predator and he would at last fly on alone.

Such apparent devotion between partners has no time to ripen in the hectic springtime of ducks. Filled with the energy of the season, they explode upon the Platte River Valley in a frenzy of splashing, posturing, calling, and chasing that began in the closing weeks of winter. Their antics are in marked contrast to the decorous rituals of the cranes, and the brilliant plumages of the males heighten the contrast. Beside them the cranes seem dull looking, with little or no outward difference between the sexes—but then the cranes are monogamous and need not search for new mates each spring. Indeed, throughout the bird world, the most striking birds in appearance and displays are usually the least likely to remain with a single mate.

Like most other short-lived birds, ducks seek new partners every year. The showy plumage of the male (or drake; the female is called a duck or hen) serves as a visual aid in the fierce competition they face in mating. Mallard and Northern Pintail drakes have distinctive markings and rich color that make it easy for the observer—avian or human—to discern their species and sex at a glance. By such signals, most drakes are spared the hostile rebuff a crane suffers on finding, after his initial overtures, that his would-be mate is actually another male.

But things are seldom simple in nature. Mallards and pintails face another problem. The drakes cannot always tell whether the ducks they pursue are of their own species because many females look so much alike. So the males sometimes display to ducks of the right sex but the wrong species. The burden—to avoid crossbreeding—falls to the female, who must pick the right mate, often from a field of noisy competitors.

*N*ear a bank of the Platte, a lone pintail hen is courted by half a dozen drakes, one of them a Mallard. With a low, irregular "inciting" call she identifies herself as unmated. The drakes respond in unison, as if directed by a choreographer. They muscle each other aside and press closer to her. They splash the water with their bills, lift their tails, and flex their wings to expose a bright patch of color, or speculum, on each wing. In so doing the Mallard more fully reveals himself; his distinctive posturing and calling, and his wing pattern with its blue speculum, give him away. The female notices such discrepancies, and in time the Mallard will be disqualified.

Suddenly she flies from the water, leading the flock into the sky. In tight formation the group races through turns, climbs, and dives. She stays in the point position, her suitors following her every action, calling to her again and again, their voices drifting down the sky like flutesong.

Back on the water the drakes resume their displaying. The river boils with drakes jockeying for position, their feathers flashing in the sunlight. One male after another crowds to the front of (*Continued on page 68*)

59

M. P. Kahl

How do birds communicate the messages of mating? This Red-winged Blackbird does it by flashing shoulder patches (left) that warn rival males away from his territory and invite females into it. The meadowlark (below) does the same with song. A pair of Tree Swallows trade calls on a branch (below left) but rely on aerial chase displays to forge a bond. Two female Wood Storks, formerly called Wood Ibis (opposite), communicate without making a sound; a gape alone invites a partner.

OVERLEAF: Strutting in snow, Sage Grouse cocks vie for mates in Oregon. Two of them fan their tails to lure hens from the scrub; two more brace for a stare-down that may end in wing slaps.

Jim Brandenburg. Below left: William V. Sleuter. Below right: Farrell Grehan. Overleaf: Tom and Pat Leeson

In full strutting display, a
male Sage Grouse swells the
air sacs on his breast
(opposite). Swallowing air in
three gulps, he inflates the
sacs, then expels the air in
hollow plopping sounds that
echo for hundreds of yards.
Tail fanned, wings drooping,
each cock advertises his
position in the lek, or display
arena. The dominant male
wins a territory near the lek's
center and there mates with
most of the hens.

Two cocks confront each
other (right) where their
strutting territories meet. If
neither backs down, a spat of
pecking and wing slapping
may erupt (below). Bouts end
in seconds and usually
without injury. Such bluffing
matches save many kinds of
birds from the risk and
exertion of real fights.

Wilfried Schurig. Below: Erwin and Peggy Bauer. Opposite: Jeff Foott

take his place among them. Only through prolonged fighting and posturing can the novice work his way through the ranks. After years of trial the strongest apprentice is thus in the best position to replace the master cock as he weakens with age or dies. The lek system ensures that the fittest male will fertilize the greatest number of females. When experimenters removed a master cock and chief apprentice from their display grounds, the result was near chaos. The surviving males crowded into the central part of the lek, carving it up into smaller pieces. Some females, unfamiliar with the new social order, avoided the lek altogether. And the hens that did appear found that many of the cocks were too inexperienced to mate effectively with them.

By late April the prairie chickens and other grouse have largely played out their annual drama, and only rarely does the wind convey the strange music of their courtship, a last call for the tardy to come and mate. Along the shorelines of the Platte River, the scattered feathers of molting birds cling to weeds and clumps of grass, but the big migratory push is over. Lured by the warming sun, ducks and geese have gone north, and their racket with them. One can hear the soft rush of the river again, along with the mingled song of the House Wrens, Mourning Doves, and catbirds that own the valley now.

The cranes have flown too. For weeks they have been leaving, one contingent at a time, each resolving itself into wedges, wheeling spirals, and long, undulating strings that fade from view with altitude and distance. Their journey is far from over. Some will fly northeast to Hudson Bay, some across western Canada to the Beaufort Sea. Others will fly along the crest of the Rocky Mountains, then west along the Yukon River to the Alaskan tundra or even to Siberia. All face hundreds of miles of hard travel and uncertain weather.

For other Sandhill Cranes spring is just beginning. The snow still whips through the upper reaches of Wyoming's Teton Range as the first cranes arrive from New Mexico in May. Just down the mountains, though, spring advances on the valley floor near Jackson Hole. Here the great birds, famished from their journey, alight to rummage for greens and roots around the thawing lakes and ponds. Some of the flock will nest here; others will continue flying north.

*F*rom the lakeside willows and marshes, unseen birds produce a jumble of song, a mixture of whistles and trilling—by turns cheerful and plaintive, hoarse and musical. A jaunty *sweet sweet sweet sweet ti-ti see* identifies the Yellow Warbler of the willows. Song Sparrows, from their hiding places in the shrubs and low aspens, sing a complex song of three or four short notes followed by a buzzy *tow-wee* and a closing series of trills. And from deep in the marsh comes the creaking-gate croak of the Yellow-headed Blackbird.

Each song is as distinctive as a fingerprint. By song alone it is possible to identify most species—and in some cases an *(Continued on page 80)*

Now you see it: the sudden flash of a male Buff-breasted Sandpiper's white underwing (right) amid the drab brown of the Alaskan tundra. Now the female sees it too, for by this eye-catching signal the male attracts hens to his territory in the lek. By fluttering leaps and flashes of his white undertail feathers, he leads them to a copulation site nearby. There his intensity rises to a crescendo with a display called a double-wing embrace (opposite below) that sometimes ends in copulation with every hen on the site. On the featureless tundra the hens will lay eggs that he will never see; shortly after the mating ritual the males wing their way to Argentina.

Now you hear it: the hoot of the Pectoral Sandpiper in the tundra's pervasive hush. An air sac on the male's breast makes the sound two or three times a second as he swoops by the female at grass-tip altitude. Soaring and diving, he alights at last; whining and growling, he finally approaches her in a frenzy of calling and flapping (opposite above) that may last a minute if she allows him to mount her—or a few seconds if she demurs.

By voice and gestures these sandpipers use their most conspicuous features to attract mates. By a wide variety of attention getters—the red crest of the male Ruby-crowned Kinglet, the spreading of the male American Redstart's colorful tail—birds of many species do the same.

J. P. Myers, VIREO (all)

Gary L. Nuechterlein

Western Grebes kick up a spray as they dash across the water of a Manitoba marsh in a display called rushing. Feet churning, necks arched, the birds may skitter over the surface for up to 20 yards, then abruptly dive. More displays strengthen the bond between them: bill shaking, head turning, even a special "weed dance" in which they brandish weeds pulled from the bottom.

Elaborate rites often accompany the courtship of birds—and especially of those whose sexes look alike. One such bird eyeing another, for example, probably sees few clues to the other's sex. Thus the impulse to court a mate may conflict with two other impulses—to fight or flee a rival. Grebes solve this problem with their calls; by their differing notes the male and female pair off with the proper sex before they begin to display.

Barry Ranford. Below: Gary L. Nuechterlein. Opposite: William V. Sleuter

Life begets life on a raft of bulrushes as Western Grebes copulate (opposite) at a California lake. Perched on the female's broad back, the male stretches his rump downward as the female arches hers upward. Sperm— as many as three billion at a time in some species—are transferred in the brief touch of his vent to hers.

The grebes' extremely short tails allow this straight-on alignment. Most other birds make a sidewise approach, an awkward maneuver that often ends in failure as the male falls off. He may grip the female's bill or head to aid his balance during treading, an apt term for his effort to stay on her back while stretching his tail down her side. All the while, she strains to tip her rump on its side for the crucial alignment of vents.

One by one the eggs are laid. A Pied-billed Grebe adds a third to her clutch (above) in a Saskatchewan marsh. Greenish blue when new, the egg dries to a chalky white that, in time, picks up a brownish camouflage of nest stains. Most female birds have only one working ovary and egg duct. Two would add weight, a hindrance to flight, and might even allow eggs maturing side by side to break if jarred against each other as the hen lands.

Tending an egg means more than just warming it; it must be warmed evenly. Also, the embryo within must not rest for long against the membrane that lines the shell; otherwise it may adhere to the membrane. So the egg must be turned often. A male Western Grebe rises to the need (left), turning each in the clutch with gentle care.

individual singer, for each bird may have a unique style recognizable to its mate and neighbors. Some bird species have local dialects, just as humans do. Thus a White-crowned Sparrow of the Tetons that strayed westward might sound a little like an outlander to Whitecrowns near San Francisco, even though they belong to the same species.

Birds use song much as they use movements, postures, and other signals of the breeding season—to attract and stimulate mates, to maintain or strengthen the pair bond, and to ward off competitors. The song they sing need not be beautiful or complex; the squeaking of a Common Grackle does the same work as the wonderfully elaborate melody of a Hermit Thrush. Mockingbirds and Brown Thrashers may sing for several minutes without interruption, while the male cardinal may sing for no more than five seconds at a stretch. And, like them, the cardinal is full of variety; human ears can recognize at least 28 different songs in its repertoire.

A bird's song is an audible fence. It announces to rivals that the singer's territory is taken and will be defended. That saves a lot of needless fighting, since few challengers will intrude on a territory they know is taken. Those that do intrude usually allow themselves to be chased out again with little resistance, for the sense of territory is so strong in both owner and intruder that territories seldom change hands by coup.

The songs of spring are triggered by hormones, which may swell a male bird's gonads, or primary sex glands, to 400 times their normal size and weight. The gonads of the male House Sparrow, an almost tireless singer, may grow from the size of pencil points to the size of peas. But as the season runs its course, the sparrow's hormone flow abates, his glands shrink, and his music begins to fade. This cycle is standard in the avian world, which is noisier at courting time than at any other. Though a few species, such as the mockingbird and Cactus Wren, continue singing through the winter to defend their territories, they sing less frequently then than in the spring.

For nocturnal birds, such as the Whip-poor-will and the Great Horned Owl, song is essential. They depend almost entirely on voice to locate mates and rivals. Is it any surprise that their songs are so easily recognized, or that their voices ring with such clarity over vast spaces, or that they repeat themselves so often? One Whip-poor-will was heard to repeat its call more than a thousand times without a pause.

Some birds attain the equivalent of song without even opening their mouths. The Common Nighthawk attracts a mate by diving toward the ground. The air rushes over his feathers, producing a loud *woof* or muffled *boom* as he plunges earthward. Woodpeckers tap a resounding drumroll on trees or drainpipes with their bills. And some owls supplement their songs with a sound akin to finger snapping as they clack their mandibles together.

When birds are not singing, they may be calling. Calls are a less complex language often used to convey information about food, danger, or distress. Scientists have found that different calls can produce different physiological responses: A starling's heart beats faster when it hears the recorded distress calls of its fellows than when it hears, say, a feeding call. Field Sparrows vary their calls to suit the occasion. A sparrow scolds an approaching human with a *chip-chip-chip;* but when the threat is more serious—a hawk—the sparrow cries a piercing *zeeeee,* and its associates take cover.

The American Bittern, a dweller of the marsh floor, has a pumping song whose low frequencies carry well through the dense marshes. Thus the bittern is easier to hear than to spot, for the reclusive bird keeps a low profile and is reluctant to fly even when cornered.

In the shadow of the Tetons, a bittern hides its nest in the recesses of the marsh. A more conspicuous nest takes shape across the pond, where two Trumpeter Swans have staked out a part of the marsh thick with bulrushes. Their nest, in use for several seasons, rises on the landscape like a brown haystack, with the huge white female perched on top of it. She is the primary nest builder, assisted in desultory fashion by her mate as he paddles around and pulls up reeds to place near the nest. Reaching out with her bill, she piles up the reeds until the nest rises out of the water to command a full-circle view of the surrounding marsh. Then she tramps on the reed mound until she has formed a cup in the top. Neither bird makes any attempt to hide the nest.

Swans, eagles, and other large birds have little need to hide their nests because they are usually strong enough to defend themselves and their nests against all enemies. But for smaller birds, artifice holds the key to survival, especially at nesting time. Many camouflage their nests or hide them so that only the keenest observers are likely to find them. At such deception the Calliope Hummingbird is an expert. She often shapes her nest to look like the cone of a lodgepole pine or spruce; she even positions it amid a cluster of real cones, usually beneath an overhanging branch that serves as a roof. When the hummingbird is done, the nest all but vanishes into the surroundings. Yet it has all the features birds need for reproduction. It gives the owner, the eggs, and the young a measure of safety from weather and predators. It keeps the eggs from rolling away. And, because the nest is lined with willow down or other soft materials, it insulates the eggs.

A few species of birds may return to the same nest each year, building a new one on top of the old. Because hummingbird nests are so small— barely wider than a walnut—the cumulative effect of reusing an old nest is still hardly noticeable. But for large, long-lived birds the accumulation can grow to dramatic proportions. A pair of Bald Eagles used the same hickory tree in Ohio for 35 years; their nest weighed about two tons when it finally crashed to the ground.

Other nests are not so grand. Black Skimmers and terns make nothing more than a shallow scrape on the beach. But they compensate for the risks of an open nest by gathering in huge colonies that deter predators. A Whip-poor-will builds no nest; instead the *(Continued on page 94)*

Nature's potters, Cliff Swallows mob a mud puddle in Wyoming (below). Excitement reigns; males may even try to mount females as the birds pick up mud by the beakful. One pellet at a time, pairs of swallows shape cave-like havens (right), stuck by the dozen onto cliff face or barn eave.

OVERLEAF: *Great Egrets spatter the dusk with white in a moss-draped stand of gum and cypress. Here in Georgia's famed Okefenokee Swamp, egrets gather each spring to nest in colonies high in the trees. Their courtship displays enliven the swamp; their great nests of sticks encumber the same branches year after year.*

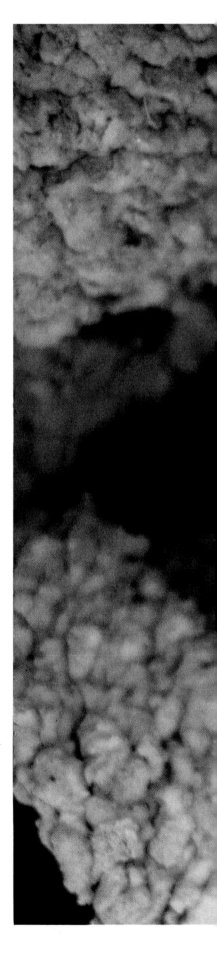

Erwin and Peggy Bauer. Right: Bates Littlehales, National Geographic Photographer

82

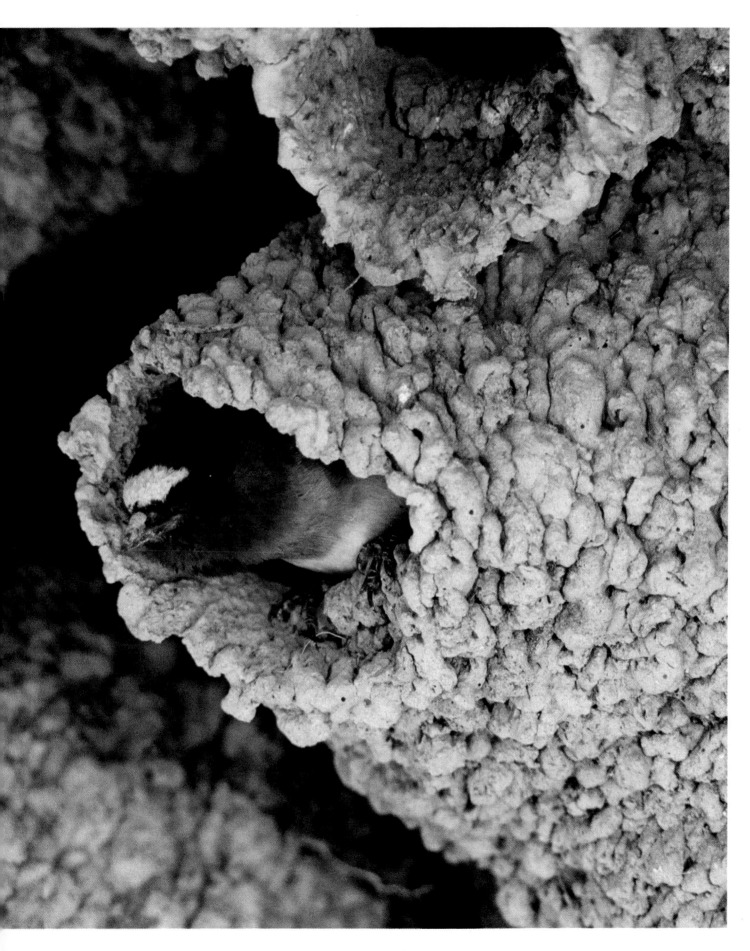

Farrell Grehan

84

Gathering hemp by a lake in Maine, a female Yellow Warbler (below) harvests material she cannot eat—a good sign that she is building a nest. In Alberta another female and her striped mate tend their nestlings (right) in a compact cup built mostly by the female. Many nests are so distinctive they identify the species of the builder.

Fred L. Knapp. Right: Keith N. Logan

Black-legged Kittiwakes cling to an Alaskan cliff (right) and warm their eggs in nests plastered to any likely niche. Both sexes build the nest, trampling bits of grass, moss, mud, and seaweed into a firm, hollowed mass.

Seabirds often breed in jam-packed colonies, a habit that makes predation more difficult. A gull's-eye view of a crag on Prince Leopold Island (opposite) shows there is safety in numbers. Thick-billed Murres spread a living blanket over this seaside parapet in the Canadian Arctic. Some 86,000 pairs have been estimated to breed on this island alone.

Like several other species, the Thick-billed Murre (below) nests on a bare surface. On a barren Alaskan ledge the female has laid a single egg. Both parents share the incubation task. Built for survival, the teardrop-shaped egg rolls in a tight circle around its pointed end when it is disturbed; a rounder egg would be more likely to roll off the ledge and smash.

Farrell Grehan. Below: Tim Thompson. Opposite: Fred Bruemmer

Nests of many shapes and sizes fill the needs of different birds. Seeking safety for their eggs and young, orioles weave hanging purses that are not hard to see but hard to reach. One of the most spectacular is the pendulous bag of the Altamira Oriole (opposite), a bird of Mexico and Central America now also nesting in southern Texas. Working from top to bottom, the female—nearly identical to her mate—weaves roots and other tough plant fibers into a sack some two feet long. The task may take her up to a month. Later, when the eggs hatch, she may enlarge the entrance at the top or tear a new one in the side.

Easy to reach but painful to raid, the nest of a Cactus Wren huddles among the forbidding spines of a cholla cactus (above) in the Arizona desert. Observers marvel at the bird's skill in bustling about the nest without getting jabbed.

Deception equals security for this female Calliope Hummingbird (right) in a conifer forest of the Pacific Northwest. Festooned with lichen scraps, her tiny cup blends well with the cone that holds it on its twig.

Lynn M. Stone. Below: Art Wolfe. Opposite: Hal H. Harrison, Grant Heilman Photography

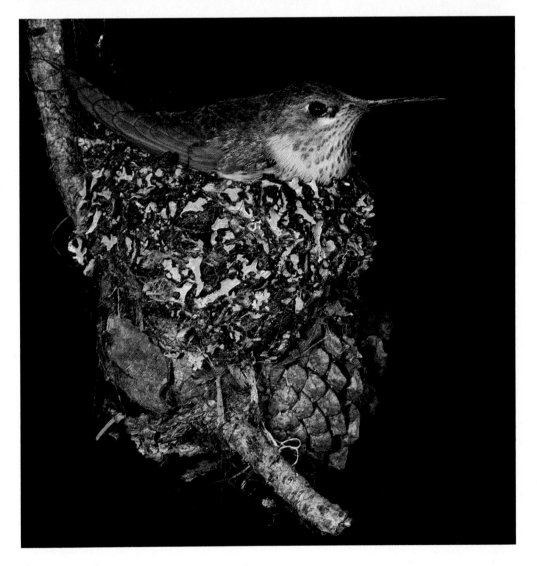

91

Arthur Swoger (all)

A nesting cavity carved out by a hard-working flicker is usurped by a starling. In a damaged tree trunk in New York City's Central Park, a male flicker labors to clean out a likely hole (opposite). Unlike most woodpeckers, the flicker has a curved bill that is ill suited to chiseling harder woods. Thus this worker chips away at a spot softened by rot, pausing now and then to gather chips by the beakful and spit them out of the opening (left). He labors in vain; the next day a starling (below) holds title. Another starling at another tree (below left) shows how it is done: Barge into the hole, knock the owner aside, and keep up the assault until the less aggressive flicker gives up and moves on. By such bullying, the European Starling has steadily spread throughout most of North America from 100 birds introduced to Central Park in 1890 and 1891.

93

Nesting without a nest, two Least Terns—smallest of the terns breeding in North America—reveal their blotchy egg in a shallow scrape on a Maryland beach. When a second egg has been laid, they will share the task of incubation. Now one bird feeds its mate a fish; in a few minutes it will probably return with another. On a hot and sunny beach, an egg may need not warming but cooling. Least Terns, like several other species, may beat the heat by splashing into the water, then shaking droplets onto the clutch.
Opposite: Michael L. Smith

clutch to be tended by the male, the second by the female.

Some birds have developed special ceremonies for changing the guard at the nest—signals of passage, perhaps, to reassure the brooding bird that all is well. Egrets exchange twigs, which may then be woven into their nests. Gannets go through a ceremony called a full greeting, in which both birds stand on tiptoe over the nest, stretch their necks, shake their bodies, point their bills skyward, touch beaks, and preen each other. That done, the bird going off duty may take a bath almost as a ritual: It skims the sea and dives through the waves, sometimes as many as 20 times in succession.

Sandhill Cranes in their incubation behavior are models of vigilance. The visitor to the arctic tundra seldom hears their familiar trumpeting, for the cranes fall silent when they begin incubating. The two sexes share the task equally, thus they are both suddenly vulnerable, tied to a small patch of tundra they cannot abandon. For a month or so it becomes the focus of their world.

One of the birds comes beating in low, a rusty shadow set against the gray Askinuk Mountains of Alaska. His mate has sat almost motionless on the nest for several hours; now she calls in recognition, her voice a low purr barely audible on the soft wind. Silently the male adjusts his course and alights some distance from the nest. The female stands stiffly, revealing two buff-and-umber eggs that glint briefly in the arctic sun. It has come down to this, all the danger and long travel of the season, now invested in these two fragile eggs that would fit in a human's palms. Without hesitating, the male steps carefully onto the nest, turns the eggs with his bill, banks the grasses more closely around the clutch to cushion it, and sits.

The female flies away to feed. When she has finished foraging, she returns to the nest. As she alights near it, one notices her brown-stained feathers and suddenly realizes that they have served their turn as camouflage, for now the tundra is green. It is almost time for hatching. The female steps to the nest, nudges her mate away, turns the eggs again, and settles on the clutch.

*I*nside one egg a chick begins its struggle toward daylight, ramming the shell with a rasp-like egg tooth on the tip of its bill. The shell that had been its haven now becomes a prison; if the chick spends too much energy trying to break out, it will die inside. A tiny crack appears in the shell. The mother hears, lifting slightly to give her youngster some maneuvering room. Again the chick punches toward the light with all its strength. More cracks. The pattern lengthens as on a sheet of shattered ice. Through the night and into the next day, the young bird punches and kicks, rests and twists, jabs and squirms until at last it forces the girdled shell apart and wriggles free. The bird lies wet and exhausted in the nest. But it is alive and hungry, warm and breathing, a tiny new crane drying in the strong sunlight of June.

*Eggs in the bank assure a
new generation of Belted
Kingfishers. Tunneling for as
much as three weeks, male
and female dig out a burrow,
usually beside a stream. A
few feet—or as many as 15—
into the bank, they hollow out
a nesting chamber. Here in
an Ohio riverbank one bird
guards its eggs (below); now
and then its mate takes a*

turn at warming them.
  *Into a burrow flies a male
with a fish for his nestlings
(opposite). During the
incubation period the male
may dig himself another
burrow and spend his nights
in it while his mate warms
their eggs.*

OVERLEAF: *Bringing a berry,
a male Cedar Waxwing feeds
his mate at their nest in a
pine in Ontario. Both birds
constructed the bulky cup; in
it she alone incubated the
eggs. Now she broods the
nestlings that both parents
share in raising.*

Ron Austing (also opposite). Overleaf: Wayne Lankinen

Foster parents raise the Brown-headed Cowbird's young in a drama played out in nests beyond counting. A favorite surrogate is the Red-eyed Vireo. In a maple in Pennsylvania a cowbird has pushed one of two eggs from a vireo's nest; now, at dawn the next day, she lays one of her own in its place (right). Later that morning the vireo laid a third; eventually she raised her two nestlings and the cowbird interloper. Often in such broods the vireo nestlings perish and only the cowbird survives. Yet studies show such parasitism does not lessen vireo numbers.

More than 100 species of birds have been known to rear the cowbird's young. In Alberta a Clay-colored Sparrow's nest (below) holds the big, brown-speckled egg of the intruder—a death sentence, perhaps, for the rightful two, since cowbird nestlings often hatch first and may later trample their nest mates or monopolize the food supply.

Parasitism is still a risky ploy. Some hosts toss out the alien egg, floor it over with new nesting material, or desert the nest. A pair of Swainson's Thrushes in Alberta did none of these; here one parent thrush feeds the foundling (opposite) alongside three of its own and later saw the whole brood feather out and fly away.

Hal H. Harrison, Grant Heilman Photography. Below: Wilfried Schurig. Opposite: Keith N. Logan

103

"Follow me!" a female Killdeer in California seems to say (right) as she flounders from her nest on the open ground, dragging a wing as if it were broken. Though not a conscious "act," the bird's performance may distract a predator with the prospect of an easy chase after an injured bird. Keeping just out of reach, she leads the intruder astray, then suddenly abandons the ruse and flies back to her vulnerable eggs (below).

Wyman P. Meinzer, Jr.   Right: William V. Sleuter

The needs of the nest keep these parent birds in Ohio coming and going. In comes greenery in the bill of a female Broad-winged Hawk (below). Observers note this behavior in some other raptors, yet its purpose remains unclear; perhaps she will use the sprig to cover the food scraps and droppings that litter the nest. Indistinct head markings suggest she is a year-old bird raising her first brood.

Out goes a fresh fecal sac in the beak of a more fastidious parent, a male Scarlet Tanager (opposite). Often a parent bird will feed a nestling, then wait for the defecation that usually follows. When birds are very young—and their digestion inefficient—the parent may eat the sac for its remaining nourishment. Later the droppings are tossed out or carried far away. Some nestlings even back up to the nest edge and save their parents the trouble.

At best it is but a meager saving in the immense toil of parenthood, the price of life that comes due each spring.

Karl H. Maslowski. Opposite: Ron Austing

The Rites of Passage

By Anne LaBastille

ar out on a mist-shrouded lake, a loon wails again and again. But on this morning in late May, his high-pitched crying elicits no reply. His mate is preoccupied with two olive brown, spotted eggs, almost twice the bulk of a chicken's, cradled in a nest of rushes and matted grasses near the water's edge.

Deep in the Adirondacks of northern New York, these Common Loons have for 29 days taken turns incubating the eggs. Yesterday signs of life stirred within one egg as a loon embryo ruptured its swaddling membrane, reaching the air chamber inside the shell, and began to breathe. Today it utters tiny sounds, and the mother responds by clucking. In this way, some scientists believe, a bond of recognition forms between mother and young before the baby birds hatch.

Now, as the sun burns through the mist, one of the eggs breaks apart. A baby loon, shaking pieces of shell from its head, emerges wet and bedraggled. The albumen rapidly dries and crumbles away, leaving a blackish brown ball of fluff with red eyes and a white belly. As soon as the second nestling struggles free of its calcareous prison, the father, having returned to the nest, carries away the shell fragments and drops them in deep water. This reduces the risk of a sharp-eyed predator locating the nest while the young are most vulnerable.

Just as prudence guides the loons' behavior on an Adirondack lake, so it is with other parent birds across the continent. During spring and summer they must nurture their young, provide for their safety, and

Fresh from the egg, a Wood Duck faces a new world. By William J. Weber.

parents—a slight shaking of the nest, air currents stirred by flapping wings, or the touch of a parent's bill on their own beaks.

Other young birds respond to their parents' special feeding calls by gaping, crying, and weaving their heads from side to side. The adults require such stimulation to start feeding their offspring. The nestlings' brightly colored mouth linings also trigger parental response and show the adults where to place the food. Finches, tanagers, and orioles display red mouth linings. Those of thrushes, wrens, and flycatchers are yellow or orange, and hole-dwelling young, such as woodpeckers, show white or yellow beak edges, probably so their parents can find them in the gloom of the nest.

If such push-button feeding behavior seems automatic, much of it is. Birds do not nourish their young out of devotion but because certain stimuli cause them to react on cue, like a whistle that brings a dog to its owner's side.

Training and learning also enter the picture as the young grow. They learn to recognize their parents and distinguish them from strange or threatening objects, just as a human infant learns to recognize its mother. Among grackle nestlings such recognition begins at the age of eight or nine days. Youngsters also quickly learn by experience which foods are edible. A juvenile Blue Jay eats a monarch butterfly, becomes ill, and spits it out. From that day forward the Blue Jay avoids all such butterflies—and their look-alikes.

Some young birds learn by copying their elders. Hawk and falcon nestlings see only dead prey brought to the nest by their parents. Lacking instinctive knowledge that living animals are potential food, the young birds develop their own prowess by watching the adults hunt. Parent Ospreys have been seen coaxing their young to fend for themselves by dropping fish in midair. Over and over the fledglings dived after the falling fish, missed, and were forced to snatch their prey from the water. Finally they began fishing alone.

Belted Kingfishers use a similar technique to train their offspring. Parents at first carry prey into their nest—a narrow tunnel burrowed into a stream bank—and deliver the fish headfirst so the nestlings will not choke on the spines. Soon the little kingfishers grow too big for their home. Climbing out onto a nearby limb, they watch their parents drop half-dead fish into the water until, driven by hunger, the youngsters splash down to retrieve the food. After about ten days a young kingfisher is ready to hunt for its own meals.

An Anna's Hummingbird in Oregon attempted to show her fledgling how to drink from a bottle feeder filled with sugar water. When the young bird was unable to locate the opening, the mother hovered beside it, probing the feeder with her beak until the youngster got the idea. She then led it to another feeder and repeated the maneuver until the fledgling had learned to sip by itself.

Care and feeding of the young puts enormous demands on the parents. At Chase Lake in North Dakota, American White Pelicans often fly several hundred miles in search of fish for their young. Soon after five Ovenbird nestlings hatched, their parents brought them food 27 times a day, a feeding schedule that increased to 123 deliveries a day before the brood left the nest. An exceptional pair of House Wrens fed their six nestlings 491 meals in a single day.

Although young birds normally get enough water from their food, species that live in hot, dry climates may require additional liquids. In some cases the parents fly to the nearest water and, after soaking belly and leg feathers, return to the nest so their young can drink from the wet plumage. Ravens sometimes offer water to their young, beak to beak.

Because baby birds come into the world with imperfectly functioning body thermostats, they must be protected from undue heat or cold. Thus the parents of newly hatched birds are faced with another task— brooding. At night or on chilly days the adults act as blankets for the young. On hot, sunny days the parents serve as parasols, shading their nests with outstretched wings.

An unprotected nestling, exposed to 90°F temperatures, will cook in minutes. Baby pelicans keep cool by the evaporation of the moist guano they and the parents spread over their bodies. Storks and New World vultures keep cool by defecating on their own naked legs and feet. Adult Wood Storks take long drinks of water, then return to the nest and spit on their young, cooling them with a shower.

Another way a bird, baby or adult, loses body heat is by fluttering the pouch on its throat—known as the gular membrane. This forces air to circulate in the lungs and the connecting sacs that extend throughout its body. This method of air conditioning is favored by species with bald gular pouches—pelicans, cormorants, frigatebirds, all of which shade their pouches by facing away from the sun when they flutter them.

As the young begin to feather out, a process that takes a week or two for birds hatched naked, the adults' brooding duties gradually diminish. Each pimple on the nestling's body gives rise first to down, later to a feather. When the feathers emerge, each rolled tightly in its own horny sheath, the down sheds off in tatters and patches. In a matter of days the quills burst from the sheaths and spread out in an orderly fashion, transforming the ungainly nestling into a sleek, efficient flying machine.

In its new plumage a young bird knows innately how to preen and oil its feathers. Loon chicks only a few hours old have already mastered a rolling preen, in which they groom their feathers while lying sideways in the water, like a sailboat keeling over, exposing their white underparts. A bird preens with its bill, grasping the base of a feather and rubbing it carefully toward the tip to remove dirt, parasites, and old oil. Preening also locks feather barbs smoothly together.

Keeping the nest clean, another important job for all birds, helps prevent plumage from becoming matted with waste. Magnolia Warblers and White-crowned Sparrows, for example, regularly eat or carry away fecal pellets deposited by their nestling—up to 67 trips a day in the case of one sparrow family. (*Continued on page 122*)

Graceless and ugly as it emerges from the egg, a baby American White Pelican relies on constant care from its parents during the first few weeks of life. The nestling acquires a fine coat of white down within about ten days. Roughly two weeks later it joins other youngsters in a social and protective group known as a pod.

Appeasing a young pelican's appetite is full-time work for the parents (right), which feed each baby some 150 pounds of fish by the time it is nine weeks old. The young bird weighs more than its parents when it leaves their care.

Jim Brandenburg (also right)

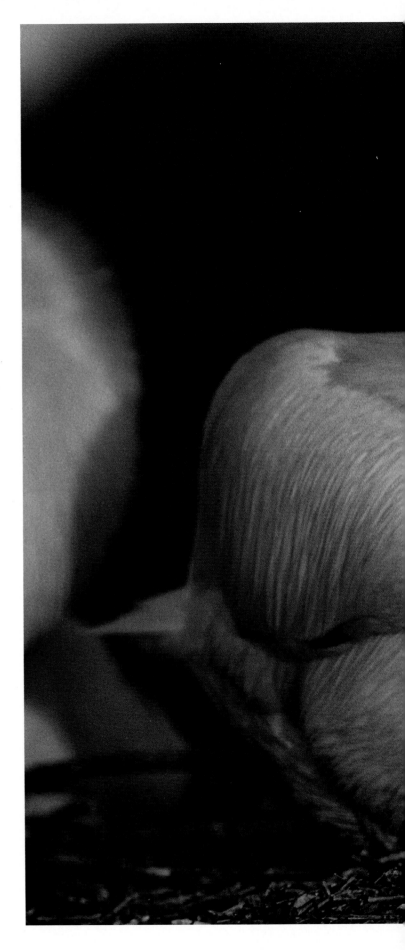

Death comes to the rookery: A California Gull, ever alert for the chance to grab a meal, seizes a young pelican. Any young bird lives in peril; among most species, only a few of the nestlings survive. At this North Dakota site, only one of four babies will reach maturity. Most others fall prey to gulls or are abandoned by parents so skittish that any disturbance can make them forsake their duties. Weaker nestlings, bullied aside at mealtimes and relentlessly attacked by older brothers and sisters, are almost always evicted from the nest, and die. Weather, predators, or other hazards may claim victims of any age. This adult (opposite) met death from unknown causes.

Thase Daniel. Below: Jack Dermid. Opposite: William J. Weber

Coaxed from the security of its nesting box, a day-old Wood Duck pauses on the threshold of uncertainty (left). Soft kuk kuk sounds from the mother summon her brood of 10 to 12 chicks—all hatched within hours of each other the day before. Wood Ducks make their homes in tree hollows, abandoned woodpecker nests, or, as here, in man-made structures. The chicks clamber from the depths of the nest and leap to the ground or water—a drop of as much as 50 feet (below). Though breathtaking, the feat rarely injures the ducklings.

The iridescent drake (opposite) usually abandons his mate as soon as they have copulated, leaving her to tend the brood.

His colorful feathers, attractive to the drab females, make him an easier mark for predators. Such outward differences between sexes, known as dimorphism, are widespread in the avian world. The more aggressive males are almost always larger and more colorful, which gives them an advantage in claiming territory and competing for mates. But in phalaropes, a group of shorebirds, the roles are reversed—females are larger, have brighter feathers, and woo the males at breeding time.

120

But not all birds are so tidy. Some woodpeckers and kingfishers make no effort at all to keep their nests clean, allowing feces to accumulate at the bottom of the nest holes. There, if a baby bird dies and is too large for a parent to remove, it is left to rot. Nests of Great Horned Owls and many pigeons and doves become so fouled with droppings that many nestlings may fall prey to disease and vermin.

Sometimes other birds—usually unmated adults of the same species or older siblings of an earlier brood—help with feeding and nest-cleaning chores. More than 130 species are known to practice this manner of baby-sitting. In one case three female bluebirds—the mother, a nonbreeding female, and a juvenile—took care of the nestlings after the father died. Another bluebird family lost its mother to pesticides, leaving the father and two eight-week-old males to raise the young successfully.

Cooperative brooding is especially common among Scrub Jays in Florida. About half the nesting parents in a community of these gregarious birds may receive assistance in raising their young. The helpers not only perform housekeeping chores, but they also serve as lookouts for snakes and will mob would-be intruders.

Surrogate parents are thought to benefit their community. One study showed that breeding pairs with assistants from outside had larger families, raising two to three more youngsters than those produced by parents lacking such helpers.

Usually birds of one species do not attempt to raise the young of another. But it does happen. A Short-eared Owl that hatched a clutch of chicken eggs brought dead mice and decapitated birds to the chicks. A cardinal without young of its own adopted several goldfish. When the fish, accustomed to being fed by humans, rose to a pool's surface with mouths gaping, the cardinal stuffed them with worms.

Defending the nest calls for a variety of tactics. Oystercatcher parents merely flee, leaving the nestlings unattended. But the young birds know instinctively to freeze, and are so well camouflaged they almost always defy detection. Among curlews, quail, and other ground nesters, the entire family freezes—and often escapes notice. American Woodcocks and Spotted Sandpipers also flee the nest, clutching their young between their legs as they fly. Many waterfowl grab the young in their bills or whisk them onto their backs before swimming to safety.

Other birds mob or dive on interlopers—or put on impressively ferocious displays. One pair of loons in Minnesota rushed to within 20 feet of canoeists who had captured their chick. Rearing up, the shrieking parents treaded water, beating the surface with outspread wings as they raced around the canoe. The moment the little loon was put back in the water, the parents dashed to its side and escorted it away.

The fulmar, a stocky seabird whose name means "foul gull" in Icelandic, wields an unusually potent weapon—as do its tube-nosed cousins, the shearwaters and petrels. Young fulmars, like their parents, store a vile-smelling, oily secretion in their stomachs that they vomit with great force and accuracy onto intruders, including their own parents if they approach before the nestlings recognize them.

Some parents use a similar tactic in defense of their young. Adult Turkey Vultures may allow humans to approach when their young are on the nest—but then the parents may suddenly throw up on the intruder, a highly effective defense when one considers the nature of the vulture's diet.

At times a young bird's worst enemies are members of its own family. Cannibalism, infanticide, and fratricide are not uncommon, especially among larger birds. Roadrunners may eat their youngest nestlings. Sandhill Cranes sometimes abandon or destroy eggs if another has already hatched. Such family slayings ensure at least one sibling's survival when food is scarce, leaving the strongest bird to pass on its genes through future generations. Herring Gulls recognize and feed only their own young. If a youngster wanders too far afield, it risks being pecked to death by neighboring gulls defending their nests. Nearly 70 percent of the chicks in one colony were killed this way.

Young birds often kill or starve weaker siblings. An extraordinary struggle called the Cain-and-Abel battle frequently takes place among young Golden Eagles. The older eaglet of a pair begins to peck at its nest mate, chasing it and even attempting to sit on it. Because the older nestling hatched first, it is larger, stronger, and more energetic than the younger bird, and eats most of the food brought by its parents. When the smaller eaglet inevitably dies, the parents remove it, eat it, or feed it to the surviving nestling.

Some birds abandon their young. Atlantic Puffin parents dote on their single youngster for about six weeks, bringing it an abundance of small fish each day. Then, abruptly, they leave it, for the approaching molting season demands that the adults head for open ocean before they become flightless. The young puffin, safe in its burrow, fasts for a week or so. Finally, driven by hunger, it waddles to the cliff edge, flaps awkwardly down into the cold water, and heads out to sea, where it will soon learn to dive for food on its own.

Grim as life can be at times, young birds, and sometimes adults, manage to enjoy playful moments. Young Brown Creepers often frolic by spiraling around and around the base of a tree, alighting, then flying off to chase one another. Young Prairie Falcons play a game of midair catch with cow dung, dropping a dry chunk from aloft, then swooping to grab it before it can hit the ground. Frigatebirds, gulls, terns, and other seabirds apparently play a similar game with fish. Black Vultures soar exuberantly on strong winds in mountainous terrains, riding the upslope gusts to high above the summits, then peeling off to plummet back into the valleys. Grown eagles sometimes buzz grizzlies, sheep, and deer as if for the sheer enjoyment of it.

One form of bird behavior that is not playful is brood parasitism. Females of some species habitually lay eggs in the nests of other birds, depending upon unwitting foster parents (*Continued on page 136*)

123

126

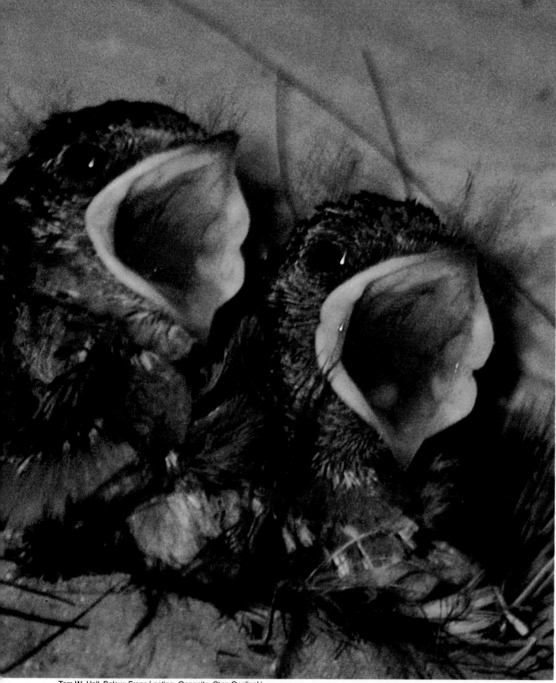

The loudest peeper gets the prize: a mouthful of insects brought by the parents of baby Barn Swallows (left). Programmed for survival, parents and young respond on cue. During the first week of life, before their eyes open, the nestlings rest motionless and silent until they feel a parent land on the rim of the nest. Then their heads pop up and their beaks stretch wide, exposing the yellow linings of their mouths. The display of color stimulates the adult to stuff the youngsters with food. Mother and father take turns feeding the nestlings, but if times are hard and foraging flights skimpy, the weakest peeper may starve.

Triggering mechanisms vary widely. For the speckle-headed young of the Western Gull (below), dinner waits behind the red spot on the adult's bill. Attracted by the color, the chick pecks at the mark and the adult regurgitates food.

Each species has a set of instinctive cues that binds parents to young so the helpless nestlings do not go hungry. But the birds can be fooled. The Horned Larks (opposite below), mistaking the photographer for a parent, begged for food. Black spots inside the nestling's bill, called directive marks, give parents a target at which to aim the meals.

Tom W. Hall. Below: Frans Lanting. Opposite: Stan Osolinski

Built for speed, this feisty roadrunner often hits 15 miles an hour in a race for food—fast enough to catch virtually any creature that moves across the desert: scorpion, lizard, snake, tarantula, or mouse. Thick, dense feathers deflect the fangs of a rattlesnake and provide insulation against scorching days and chilly nights. Short, stubby wings make the roadrunner's attempts at flight awkward and short lived, but the bird's speed and agility on the ground make it a formidable hunter. By swiveling and focusing each of its eyes independently, the roadrunner can keep one eye on the sky for hawks and one on the ground for prey. The fruits, seeds, and eggs that supplement its diet provide the bird with precious liquid. And with a digestive system that metabolizes food into water, the roadrunner gets enough moisture to survive in its arid environment.

Bruce Dale, National Geographic Photographer

Stomach juices potent enough to digest bone, hair, and feather make the roadrunner an all-purpose eater. Here, an adult seizes a luckless horned lizard, beats it to death on a rock, and crams it down a nestling's throat.

Too much to swallow, the meal comes back up (opposite). Patiently the parent feeds it to another infant and stands by until the lizard is consumed.

Wyman P. Meinzer, Jr. (all)

132

A Snail Kite hovers over a Florida lake, where the bird will pluck an apple snail from the water, pry out the meat with her sharply hooked beak, and feed it to one of her nestlings—a duty shared by her mate (below).

This bird eats about three dozen of these mollusks a day—and virtually nothing else. Such specialized tastes may doom the bird as the disappearance of marshland diminishes the snail supply. Everglade Kites, as the birds are also known, once nested throughout the state. Today only a few hundred remain in scattered spots across central and southern Florida.

James A. Kern (all)

133

Stately diners—members of the heron family—use a variety of schemes to bag a meal. Here a Snowy Egret startles its quarry into telltale movement by stirring the mud with a foot. The egret flips its catch in the air and swallows it headfirst so it will not stick in the gullet.

A Tricolored Heron (formerly Louisiana Heron) raises its wings to cast a shadow on the water (far right). This style of fishing may attract prey to the shadow or reduce surface glare, making it easier for the bird to see its victims.

William V. Sleuter (also above and below). Right: William Ervin

language of its species' courtship rituals. Song is often the key, but the song of a bird does not come naturally. Like humans learning to talk, songbirds learn gradually by listening to adults.

In the first two months of life, young birds may try to imitate their elders, producing a poor facsimile of song. The rudiments of adult song are there, nothing more. But appearances deceive. In those brief weeks the nestlings have memorized the basic song of their species, even though they cannot utter it convincingly. The pattern is set forever in their young brains. By the next year, they can sing without practice, producing trills and flourishes when they first meet prospective mates.

What else must birds learn? Which facets of life are not genetically programmed into their behavior? The ability to tell friend from foe must be learned from parents and other birds. Newly hatched birds display a trusting innocence that, as the weeks go by, inevitably changes to a general wariness. They must distinguish between enemies that they can reasonably confront and those to be avoided altogether. They must learn to fear humans—the only animal that can kill at a distance.

Young birds also must learn what *not* to fear. Those that live in relative safety, isolated on islands or in high mountains, usually grow up only mildly wary and suspicious. But birds that live where predators are present become extremely cautious. Experience soon teaches them to ignore large, loud, moving objects, such as planes and trains, that are harmless at a distance. This general loss of fear of harmless objects is called habituation.

Young birds do not have to learn how to drink or how to preen their plumage. Nor must they be taught to fly. Most birds instinctively flutter their wings when just a few days old, long before they grow their first adult feather. Eaglets on the rim of their nest and young gannets clinging to cliff edges practice flapping their wings for hours to gain strength and skill. But most other birds need no training or practice. Petrels, born and reared within burrows, simply walk to the edge of a cliff, glide alone into the night and settle on the sea. Swifts and swallows also fly expertly on their first try. Regardless of their introduction to flight, all young are adept at it soon after they take their initial leap.

*Y*oung loons, on the other hand, must gear up for their maiden flight. They practice by beating their wings on the water until, at about 12 weeks of age, they patter across the surface and, with wings and feet flapping, rise shakily into the sky. Loons learn to fly in solitude and silence on their Adirondack lake, far from the pandemonium of Bonaventure Island, 600 miles to the north.

A fog-shrouded, desolate, rocky knob thrusting 200 feet above the Gulf of St. Lawrence, Bonaventure is one of the largest Northern Gannet rookeries in all of North America. Thousands of birds nest on the rocks and cliffs—a frenzy not only of gannets but also of kittiwakes, guillemots, puffins, murres, gulls, and other seabirds. (*Continued on page 150*)

Pausing between sips of
nectar, a Black-chinned
Hummingbird hovers before
a hibiscus blossom. The
hummingbird's thin bill and
extensible tongue enable it to
reach deep inside the flower
for droplets of nectar. Slender
enough to explore a flower,
the hummingbird's bill is also
a precise and deadly weapon.
Flies, gnats, and spiders
supplement the bird's liquid
diet. Its bill, like that of any
bird, must serve as hand and
mouth, for its wings are
devoted to flight.

Designed for varied
purposes, bills come in many
shapes and sizes, from the
nine-inch mud-probe of the
Wood Stork to the fish-
grasping forceps of the
Hooded Merganser. When
the time comes to build a
home, a woodpecker's sturdy
bill serves as a chisel, a
kingfisher's as a spade.

Bills also serve as badges at
breeding time. Robins' bills
turn yellow in spring as
an indication of sexual
maturity, then revert to
brown in autumn. American
White Pelicans develop
temporary knobs on their
upper bills that may help the
birds survive the combats of
spring. Like many birds,
pelicans fight for mates and
territory by jousting with
their bills, though seldom to
the death. Some scientists
believe these horny growths
function as a target for an
adversary's blows, averting
damage to the pouch.

George D. Lepp, Bio-Tec Images

140

A Roseate Spoonbill stirs up a meal in the Florida Everglades. Wagging its head from side to side, the bird probes the muddy water with its paddle-shaped bill. Sensitive tissue in the broad tip makes the bird's bill a subtle underwater snare. At the touch of a fish, shrimp, or insect, the bill snaps shut.

E. R. Degginger

141

Bills are specialized for all manner of eating. A tiny red vise, a cardinal's bill makes short work of a seed (opposite). Rows of bristles, like a misplaced mustache, help the shoveler strain plankton and insects from the water (below). The Red Crossbill (lower left) pries open the scales of pinecones with the overlapping tips of its bill. Insects disappear down the maw of the Chuck-will's-widow, which plies the night skies with its mouth agape. A fringe of bristles along the inside of its bill (lower right) probably helps sweep in food.

OVERLEAF: *The Black Skimmer's scissors sweep through the shallows for fish. When the blades find a victim, the skimmer nabs the fish and flips it down the hatch.*

Gary R. Zahm. Below left: William Ervin. Below right: William J. Weber. Opposite: Steve Maslowski

Overleaf: Steven C. Wilson and Karen C. Hayden, Entheos

Refined by the ages, a bird's eyes function at a level of perfection unmatched in the animal kingdom. Birds use keen sight—their most highly developed sense—to find food and spot adversaries.

When startled, a Least Bittern points its narrow bill skyward and freezes, while its eyes stare straight ahead toward danger (opposite).

A shrike can discern a bumblebee at 300 feet and snatch it on the wing with lethal precision; a Golden Eagle dives toward a rabbit at 150 miles an hour, keeping its victim always in focus.

The eyes of night-hunting owls are packed full with light-gathering cells, which help them locate prey. And a supple neck compensates for

the owl's limited field of view; this Barred Owl (lower) can rotate its head 270 degrees. Like all birds, the Sandhill Crane (upper) has an extra "eyelid"—or nictitating membrane—that helps clean and moisten its eyeball; it may also act as a windscreen during flight.

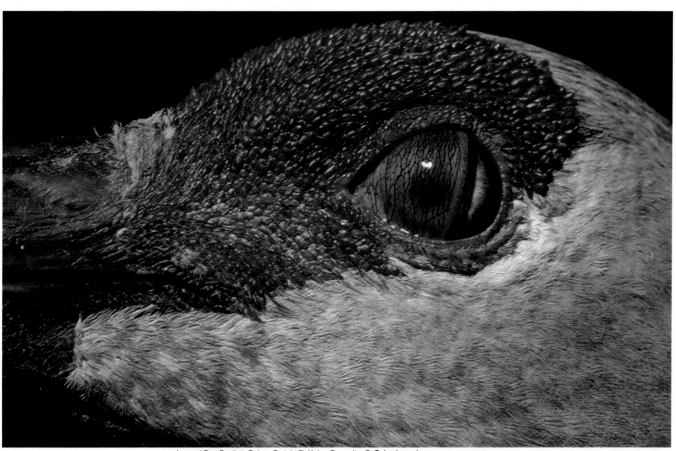

Jen and Des Bartlett. Below: Dwight R. Kuhn. Opposite: C. C. Lockwood

What goes up must come down—many birds spend a good deal of time perching and walking. The Purple Gallinule virtually walks on water, its spindly toes transforming lily pads into floating flagstones (right). For the Red-footed Booby (below), flexible paddles serve for perching on branches or propulsion on the high seas.

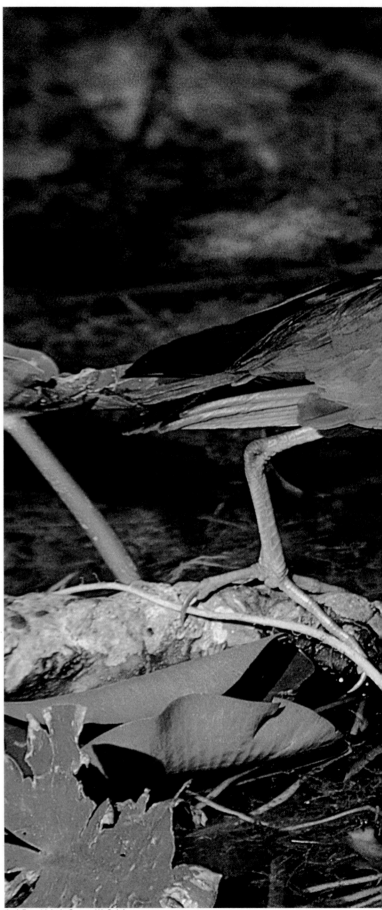

Jack Dermid. Left: George W. Calef

148

shearwaters will die of thirst if offered only fresh water to drink. Other birds, including puffins, auks, and some penguins, can tolerate either fresh or salt water.

Water can also play a part in a bird's feeding habits. Common Grackles will dunk peanut butter or doughnuts into birdbaths before offering the food to their young. The American Dipper, an aquatic songbird of the western United States, walks, dives, or flies into icy, swift-flowing mountain streams, maneuvering through rapids and clinging to the bottom as it searches for insects, worms, mollusks, and water bugs. Many gulls, while on the wing, swoop down to catch fish at the water's surface; one Great Black-backed Gull snatched a fish away from a shark.

A Cooper's Hawk once put water to use in a bizarre but effective way: The hawk, according to a witness, carried a violently struggling starling "into a depression where several inches of rainwater had collected. Once in the water with the starling, the hawk merely stood on top of it for about four or five minutes, by which time the starling appeared to be dead. Then the hawk flew easily away, the starling in its grasp."

In summer many birds must stay close to water as they renew worn or lost plumage. Molting is a vulnerable time for ducks, geese, swans, grebes, and other species, for they shed all of their old flight feathers at once, grounding them for a few weeks. For adults a complete molt means that almost every feather will be replaced with a new one. Usually birds molt twice a year. For loons, flight feathers are molted only once a year so they can migrate in the autumn. Many birds carry fewer feathers in summer than in winter, for the same reason humans shed coats.

Different species molt at different times, usually in the breeding area after the young have become self sufficient or after the fall migration. Such timing gives birds a rest from other high-energy demands. Molting requires great energy output because a bird's feathers, made of protein, can account for more than 7 percent of its total weight. To satisfy protein requirements when molting, even nonmigratory species may increase their daily food consumption by about one-fourth.

The loons that summered on their Adirondack lake will not molt until they arrive at winter quarters—as near as the New Jersey coast or Chesapeake Bay, as distant as the Gulf of Mexico. Loons that migrate build up body fat to use as fuel for the trip south. But their needs are not as great as those of their neighbors, the Magnolia Warblers. Before leaving for their long journey to Central America, the warblers increase their body weight by about 30 percent.

As September fades into October, the Adirondacks begin to cool. Food supplies dwindle. The loons increasingly feel a restlessness. The young, now grown to nearly adult weight and size, look to the changing sky, so full of unknowns, yet so compelling. Then one November morning, obeying some mysterious clock, they set off across the water, climb above the morning mist, and are gone.

A Flammulated Owl lands softly at its nest in the Colorado Rockies, bearing a caterpillar for its offspring (below). Soon the nestling will outgrow its home, once a nursery for flickers.

Summer always brings the transition from nest to open air. A chubby trio lines up for another meal outside the nest (right). Young owls remain under their parents' care as they wait out the fledging period that leads to their first cloak of feathers and, finally, to flight.

Art Wolfe (also right)

154

Flanking their mother, four Great Horned Owls huddle in their nest. This large family is a rare one— only an owlet or two usually survive the first weeks of life.

Two months after hatching, the young owls make their maiden flight—an awkward swoop toward the ground. But for weeks after they have fledged, the young stay near the nest, screaming for food with cries variously described as "hair raising" and "blood curdling."

As autumn approaches, the owlets lose their fear of squirrels and rabbits, which in time have good reason to fear the young fliers. The birds soon master their hunting tools—silent wings, powerful talons, sensitive hearing, and keen vision— which make them lords of the night woods.

Keith N. Logan

Wings Across the Sky

By Frank Graham, Jr.

wo dozen men and women, warmly dressed against the chill wind of early October that sweeps across the island from the North Atlantic, make their way through an old field partly grown up to bayberry and shadbush. Occasionally they stop to focus their binoculars on a mixed flock of warblers and vireos flitting through the dense shrubs. When the birds briefly outdistance them, they quicken their pace.

"There—at one o'clock in the bayberries!" one of the birders calls. "Blackpolls and Cape Mays. And a Blackburnian—you can still make out the color on his throat!"

The birders, almost running now, emerge into a clearing as they try to keep the warblers in sight. They lift their binoculars again. And there, sharply in focus and staring straight back at them . . . another dozen birders hotly stalking the same quarry.

It would not be accurate to write that bird watchers are as numerous as birds in early fall on Block Island, but their numbers do rise and dwindle in proportion to the flood of migrants in passage from the north. On this day the fall migration was at high tide. A strong northwest wind, arising the night before, had pushed ahead of it the millions of small birds following the coast of Maine from the Maritime Provinces and northern New England. The same wind had pushed off course other flocks traveling along the shoreline.

As dawn broke, the birds found themselves over open water, many miles off the New England coast. Suddenly a fragment of land appeared

Arctic Terns, marathon migrants, hover in a cloudy sky. By Entheos.

out of the sea. A shower of birds—tanagers, warblers, thrushes, flycatchers, vireos, plovers, and sandpipers—descended on Block Island. They will remain there, feeding and resting, until favorable weather conditions once more spur them on the next leg of their long journey to a sunnier land.

Block Island, which lies ten miles off the coast of Rhode Island, offers an almost unrivaled stage on which to observe the dramatic pageant of migration. A part of New England, Block Island's history is all of a piece with the rich heritage of bird lore built up over two centuries by the region's poets, painters, and naturalists. Longfellow played on his compatriots' emotional tie to birds:

Think of your woods and orchards without birds!
Of empty nests that cling to boughs and beams
As in an idiot's brain remembered words
Hang empty 'mid the cobwebs of his dreams!

Block Island's 11 square miles of fields and cliffs stand like a beacon athwart the sea-lanes over which the winds of autumn have sped migrating birds for thousands of years. There the spectacle is breathtaking when the hosts of birds build up as they await the next propitious wind. The dense forests that often conceal songbirds in their summer or winter homes are absent for the most part on this island, where settlers cleared the land for farms 300 years ago. Warblers land on neatly clipped lawns, tanagers perch on stone walls, and Merlins patrol the open cliffs in search of exhausted smaller birds they may kill and eat before continuing the journey south.

This concentration of migrants also is helping scientists unravel long-standing questions about migration. A woman who bands birds on the island struggles to keep up with the torrent of warblers that entangle themselves in the nearly invisible mist nets she has set up between clumps of shrubbery.

Extricating each bird in turn from the nets, she takes it into a tiny laboratory in her family's home. There she weighs and measures it and affixes a small, numbered aluminum band to one of its legs before releasing it to continue its journey south. If any of the banded birds is found in the future, it will help scientists to piece together the details of that species' migratory routes. This birdbander recently spoke about her findings to a group of autumn visitors at her makeshift laboratory.

"Here's a Blackpoll Warbler," she said, holding up a bird, perhaps five inches in length from beak to tail, she had just removed from a mist net. The yellows and olive greens of its fall plumage revealed no trace of the black cap that distinguishes males in breeding condition and gives the species its name. "It weighs about half an ounce, and when I push aside its feathers, I can see it has built up deposits of fat—some ornithologists call them 'fuel tanks'—as reserves for migration. I've captured some Blackpolls that weigh almost an ounce. They are so fat they look as if they will burst! But a tiny bird like this needs a lot of fuel if it is going to fly all the way to South America."

Across the continent a similar flow of birds toward the tropics takes place. The hills and palm-fringed beaches around Santa Barbara, California, serve as counterparts to Block Island's rolling fields. Migrants that normally use the briefly flowering deserts for respite on the flight north in spring now shun those dry, flowerless regions in the fall and hug the more hospitable coastline. South-flying birds, such as Wilson's and Townsend's Warblers, descend on Santa Barbara about the time other species, such as Water Pipits, are arriving to spend the winter.

Subtle environmental conditions seem to influence the size of migrant flocks along the coast. On overcast nights the birds may drift over the water because they cannot see the contour of the land below. At daylight they come down through the clouds, see water, and head back to the coast, arriving in droves.

Along the west coast, as in other regions of North America, there is great diversity in the behavior of migrants. Some Townsend's Warblers may stop for the winter anywhere from northern California down to Santa Barbara. This is a bird of the forests, nesting in the northern woods and wintering in a similar habitat farther south. Some Townsend's Warblers settle in around Santa Barbara, last stop before the barren terrain that lies beyond. Those that do not linger in Santa Barbara must fly on over the extensive scrublands and deserts of southeastern California and northwestern Mexico until they reach the mountain forests of the Sierra Madres of Mexico and Central America.

One of the species that southern California's birders look for in the fall is the Elegant Tern. This seabird, with its slender orange bill, long black crest, and immaculate white breast and throat, is appropriately named. Before the 1950s it was seldom seen in California. But about that time the birds began wandering north from their colonies in Mexico after the breeding season. Today these reverse migrants are fairly common in southern California, beginning to arrive in July. Some even fly as far north as San Francisco. By late fall the birds leave California for their native subtropical waters in Mexico.

The power of flight, which confers so many advantages, exacts an enormous price in expended energy. Migration is one way birds deal with the problem of replenishing that energy, keeping themselves at all seasons in touch with abundant supplies of food. Of the 650 or so species that breed regularly in North America, nearly 80 percent migrate to some extent. No other aspect of bird behavior makes us so aware of the fragility of their lives, or leaves us with such a lasting sense of their adaptability and hardiness in what is often a hostile environment.

Some birds, such as prairie chickens and cardinals, seldom stray more than a few miles from their breeding territories. Others take part in long flights only occasionally. Ornithologists call these irregular movements irruptions rather than true migration. Irruptions are characteristic of crossbills, redpolls, and many owls, all residents of the far north that may fly southward when their winter food runs short. Evening Grosbeaks also move irregularly, and in some years a portion of their midwestern breeding population flies not south, but east to the Atlantic states.

Altitudinal migration occurs annually among some species. Various jays, juncos, and chickadees, after their breeding season high in the mountains of the far west, fly to lower elevations as cold weather comes on, while Mountain Quail *walk* down the slopes single file in little groups of 10 to 30. The eider ducks of Canada swim on their migration, often covering great distances.

Bird migration is, in its own way, as regular as the movement of the tides and the wheeling of the planets. In fact, the term was defined rather exhaustively by the French ornithologist Jean Dorst as "a series of periodic 'round-trips'—usually annual—in the course of an animal's life cycle between a breeding area—called 'home'—and a region where the animal spends a period of varying length outside the reproductive area and which it then leaves to go back to its 'home.' "

Dorst did well to put quotation marks around the word home. Nearly a century and a half ago, Henry David Thoreau described the Scarlet Tanager as "the surprising red bird, a small morsel of Brazil, advanced picket of that Brazilian army" in the New England woods, and only recently have ornithologists caught up with this concept. North Americans are being chauvinistic when they refer to "their" tanagers, warblers, and vireos leaving home temporarily to winter in the tropics. It would be more correct to describe these birds as residents of the tropics that fly north for a short time each year to mate and raise their young.

Nearly a quarter of the land and freshwater birds that breed north of Mexico, about 150 species, live elsewhere for most of the year—in Mexico, Central America, South America, and the West Indies. Many warblers stay on their breeding grounds for only about three months. They spend two to three months on migration, and the rest of the year, perhaps six or seven months, on their winter range.

Scientists put forth at least two major theories to explain migration. According to one theory, most of our migrants were originally northern birds that were driven south during the Pleistocene epoch as the glaciers advanced across the Northern Hemisphere. As the glaciers retreated some 10,000 years ago, birds began to move back into their former territory to find sufficient food to raise their young. Because the northern winters became harsher than in preglacial times, these "northern" birds were forced south again at the end of each summer.

The other theory regards most of our migrant birds as tropical in origin. Because of the lushness of the tropics, the bird population exploded, and some species had difficulty finding enough food for their young. In the wake of the retreating glaciers, they gradually pushed northward. This annual invasion enabled migrant birds to prey on the enormous flush of insects in the north and gave the birds longer periods of daylight in which to eat.

Many ornithologists find these two theories in general to be compatible. Hummingbirds, orioles, tyrant flycatchers, and several other groups of birds are clearly of southern origin. Other migrant birds, such as many sandpipers and plovers, may have originated in the Arctic regions. Yet each species has evolved its own migratory patterns and routes on these broad foundations.

Migration exacts a price while conferring advantages. Ornithologists who studied a population of Dark-eyed Juncos centered in Michigan and Indiana assessed some of the risks of migration. In general the males in this population wintered farther north than the females, which tended to migrate to southern states, such as Alabama and South Carolina. The males that remained in the north suffered high losses during harsh weather, but many of the females that braved the hazards of long-distance travel also were killed.

If the phrase "the mysteries of migration" has become a cliché, it remains especially apt. There is simply a great deal we still do not know about the reasons and mechanics of bird migration. We share to some extent in the ignorance of our ancestors who were puzzled by the abrupt disappearance of many familiar species when summer came to an end. To what dim countries had they flown? In northern Europe early naturalists speculated that swallows and other small birds hibernated like frogs in the mud beneath ponds. More imaginative souls ventured the theory that birds flew away each fall to the moon.

As human mobility increased, the migrants were tracked to their winter quarters, but other aspects of the phenomenon we call migration remain matters of speculation. For instance, what triggers migration? Scientists originally believed that the onset of cold weather and dwindling food supplies sent our summer residents packing. Yet, in most cases, the migrants leave well before those hardships occur. Swallows often depart while the late summer air is still alive with midges and other tiny insects.

Here, as in the case of the origins of migrants themselves, there is a mix of answers. External forces mingle with internal ones to prepare birds for their twice-yearly travels. The longer days of March and April play a vital role for many species. Reacting to this gradually increasing light, internal organs, such as the pituitary and pineal glands, stimulate the swelling of the sex glands. Restlessness overwhelms each bird, which feeds voraciously to build up deposits of fat that will carry it through the long ordeal ahead.

But changing light does not apply in all cases. Birds that winter in equatorial regions, where the hours of daylight vary little, if at all, also undergo physiological changes when time comes for their return trip north in spring. Changes in rainfall, wind direction, and temperature may affect their departure schedule, but no single factor explains precisely why they leave when they do. Perhaps some internal clock, set in motion by the eons of each species' evolutionary history, prompts the birds to fly north again at the appointed time.

Whatever the trigger, birds alter their behavior at the end of the breeding season when their young have flown. (*Continued on page 170*)

Laura Riley. Below: Jeff Foott. Opposite: Anthony Mercieca, Photo Researchers

Prepared for winter, a stay-at-home Acorn Woodpecker (opposite) sits amid the nuts his communal group has stored in a California pine tree. While other birds migrate, these industrious residents of the west and southwest drill holes in oaks, pines, and sycamores, then tamp an acorn into each cache. They also stash food in utility poles, house walls, and fence posts (below). One giant sycamore in California had 20,000 storage holes drilled in it. With their sharp beaks drilling at high speed, Acorn Woodpeckers work in groups of two to ten to excavate even larger holes for nests.

Another diligent hoarder, the White-breasted Nuthatch (above) is eager and agile enough to catch a falling nut in midair.

How do birds remember where the food is stored? Jays may not, as evidenced by the sprouting of oaks where forgetful birds have buried acorns. But the Clark's Nutcracker, a master hoarder that may bury more than 30,000 pine seeds in a season, can retrieve its stockpiles months later. Studies suggest that nutcrackers use landmarks to locate caches.

Bill Dyer

Bill Dyer, Photo Researchers

Changing colors with the seasons, a male Scarlet Tanager (far left) wears black and bright red plumage for nesting and breeding. In courting, he spreads his wings to show off his scarlet back. Females respond by whistling. By late summer a molting male tanager (left) changes to olive and yellow, but some red remains. By fall a male migrating to South America assumes a winter plumage of greenish yellow (below), which serves as his camouflage in the jungle.

Like the tanager, other birds regularly replace their worn-out feathers, timing the change to meet the special needs of the season.

John Trott

In most cases the barriers that each mated pair had put up against other individuals of their own kind during breeding begin to crumble. Abandoning their heightened suspicion and aggression, they become gregarious once again. They join in flocks, which often include several species—birds such as warblers and sparrows that may display similar patterns of feeding or flight, forming a single, loosely organized group.

Flocking holds several advantages. Large concentrations of shorebirds, for example, may intimidate potential predators or confuse them by their complex, evasive tactics. Canada Geese flying in V-formation conserve energy by using the lift of disturbed air created by the beating wings of the bird ahead. Young birds on their first migration may benefit from joining flocks that include experienced adults.

Whooping Cranes are especially solicitous of their young on migration. One or more families make up the flocks that depart in fall from their nesting grounds in northwestern Canada. The white-and-rust-colored young fly and feed with their parents on the long, hazardous flight to the Gulf coast, where family ties persist through the winter and often on the flight north again the following spring.

The actual moment of departure from the breeding grounds, like the preparations leading up to it, differs from species to species. Weather plays a dominant role, as the restless flocks wait for favorable conditions before setting off. Each species has also evolved over thousands of years a distinct migratory route, having shaped it according to its own capabilities and the demands of the environment.

The Arctic Tern's migratory pattern is one of the wonders of the natural world. This graceful seabird, long winged and swallow tailed, flies more than 12,000 miles—*twice* each year. Some nest within the Arctic Circle, then fly south to Antarctic waters for the winter, which of course is summer in the Southern Hemisphere.

Details of the Arctic Tern's fall migration began to be revealed during the 1920s, when ornithologists visited their northern breeding islands and placed aluminum bands on the legs of thousands of individuals. Later recoveries of some of the banded terns enabled ornithologists to plot their routes. Terns from colonies in New England and the Maritimes fly northeast in autumn to link up south of Greenland with others flying down from arctic colonies.

The terns then follow a great-circle route across the Atlantic, skirting Iceland and the northern British Isles. From there they fly directly south, past Spain and the western coast of Africa. Many of the terns follow the African coast all the way to Antarctica. Other flocks fan out over the Atlantic to continue their southward journey off the South American coast. Meanwhile, still other Arctic Terns that nest in northwestern Canada migrate south along the western coastlines of North and South America. All are traveling in search of their staple food, the crustaceans that live only in the cold waters of the Arctic and subantarctic regions. Whatever the route they take, birds of this species experience more hours of daylight than any other birds on earth.

Through numerous experiments, ornithologists have gained great appreciation for the ability of birds to find their way around the globe.

During the 1950s European scientists captured large numbers of starlings on their fall migration through Holland. The starlings were transported to Switzerland, where they were banded and released. The adult birds quickly reoriented themselves and flew to their customary winter quarters in the British Isles and northern France. But the young starlings continued in the same direction as they had started, and failed to compensate for their displacement. They landed in Spain, Portugal, and southern France. The lesson here: The adults had learned the location of their winter quarters and used true navigation to get there. Their young seemed to have relied solely on a preset compass direction.

Manx Shearwaters have performed even more puzzling feats. Biologists took some of these medium-size seabirds from their nesting burrows on Skokholm Island off Wales and released them in distant places. Although birds of this species will not ordinarily fly over land, a Manx Shearwater released in Italy headed northwest over the Alps and returned to its burrow on Skokholm. Later, a shearwater removed from a British nesting colony and taken across the Atlantic to Boston found its way home in $12\frac{1}{2}$ days—faster than a letter sent from Boston with news of its release!

Each migrant must solve, under natural conditions, the problems scientists posed for those starlings and shearwaters: Where am I? Where do I want to go? How do I get there? Some birds undoubtedly rely partly on natural landmarks with which they have become familiar on migration. But if a Manx Shearwater can fly 3,000 miles across an ocean, starting from a place it has never seen before, and locate its own burrow among thousands of others on a small island, it must be credited with uncanny skills as a navigator.

Scientists are trying to understand the mechanism of those skills by devising controlled experiments. Working with starlings and other small birds in cages, researchers tested the birds' sense of direction. On spring days starlings faced northeast, then northwest, and in the fall they faced southwest, the usual directions in which they would migrate. But when scientists used mirrors to change the direction of sunlight entering the cages, the starlings were thrown off course. Similar experiments in planetariums, in which researchers altered the patterns of stars overhead, confused birds that ordinarily migrate at night.

So, for daytime migrants, the sun plays an important role in navigation. The stars are equally important for night fliers. But a bird must know where it is in relation to other points before it can make effective use of the sun or stars. And what does a bird use for a compass when the skies are densely overcast?

One of the most popular theories concerns the role of the earth's magnetic field. This field is strongest at the poles and weakest at the Equator. Obviously, instruments of marvelous sensitivity are required to detect and make use of the magnetic field. Is it possible that the birds

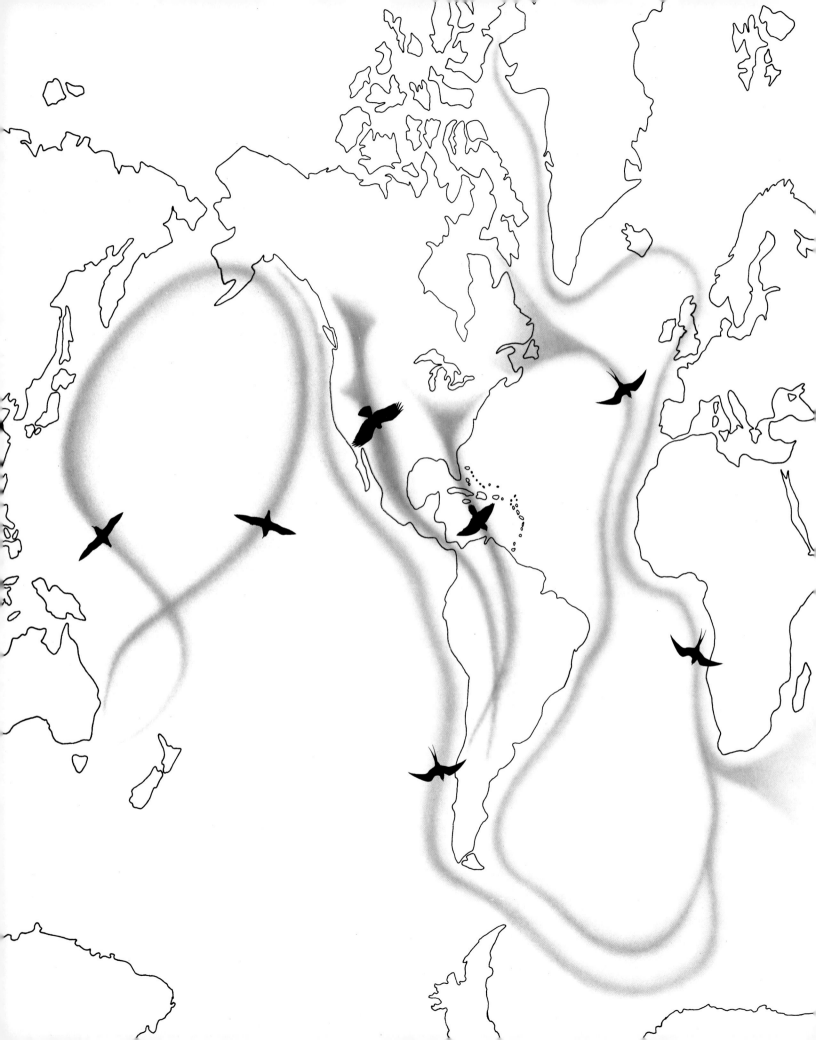

Incredible travelers include Arctic Terns, which fly to the ends of the earth (blue route); Short-tailed Shearwaters (purple), which loop over the Pacific; and Swainson's Hawks (green) and Bobolinks (gold), which commute annually between North and South America. (See map supplement for other routes.)

OVERLEAF: *Aligned in the familiar V-formation, flocks of Snow Geese migrate south over California. Each bird gets a lift from the air roiled by the bird ahead. Older and stronger birds usually take the lead; younger or weaker ones frequently hang back in the slipstream, where the flying is easier.*

Opposite: Map by Rob Wood. Silhouettes by Carl Mukri. Overleaf: Frans Lanting

have some internal compass that keeps them on the proper course? Some recent studies suggest they may. A scientist at Cornell University has found iron-rich tissue in the heads of pigeons. Whether this provides a clue to how birds navigate accurately in the absence of sun, stars, or physical landmarks is not yet known, but there is some intriguing supporting evidence. To learn whether the birds were affected by magnetic iron deposits, the scientist released several homing pigeons at a huge magnetic anomaly in Rhode Island called Iron Mine.

The birds lost their way. But once clear of the magnetic area, they recovered their bearings and flew on the correct course once more. Other experiments with pigeons have shown that the severity of the birds' disorientation near such anomalies depends on the strength of the magnetic pull. If the deposit is a large one, the pigeons are more confused than if it is a small one.

None of these theories about the ways birds navigate is wrong. It is apparent now that birds use many sources of navigational information and the scientists' beliefs are complementary. The next step is for scientists to discover how these various cues function in relation to each other. Which are dominant? How does the ability to handle these cues develop in different birds?

Another question that has gone unanswered for a long time concerns the numbers and flight paths of night migrants. Only with the recent development of sophisticated technology, such as radar, have scientists begun to come up with detailed answers.

A team of Swarthmore College researchers used radar to track migrants off the Atlantic coast. Watching radar screens on which the birds showed up as streaks and dots, the team followed the flight of millions of shorebirds, warblers, and other birds that flew south from Cape Cod and Nova Scotia, bound for the coast of South America. Most of the migrants flew the distance nonstop in about 86 hours. From the North American coast to Bermuda, they flew at about 6,500 feet. On a southeast tack from there, they gained altitude, passing over Antigua at 21,000 feet. Near Tobago they began their gradual descent to the South American mainland.

Analysis of compass headings indicates that a remarkably simple guidance system keeps the birds on a steady course during this 3,000-mile flight. After the birds leave North America, they fly southeast until they reach Bermuda. There they must adjust course and turn southwest or be swept out to sea. But they do not purposely change heading—the trade winds from the Sargasso Sea push them on their way toward the South American continent. Substantial evidence supports the idea that these birds, like many others, can establish and maintain a compass heading from the sun, the stars, or the earth's magnetic field.

This flight, which may include up to 12 million birds on a favorable night, is the longest nonstop journey (Continued on page 180)

173

A Blackpoll Warbler (right) finds his trip to South America delayed by a nylon mist net at a birdbanding station in West Virginia. At the same station a bander (below) has his hand full processing two Tennessee Warblers and one Black-throated Blue Warbler. Captured birds are quickly identified, weighed, measured, affixed with leg bands, and then released. Information inscribed on the bands enables scientists and bird watchers worldwide to trace the birds and thus study the mysteries of their behavior and migration. Still, no one has adequately explained how the tiny Blackpoll Warbler, weighing less than an ounce, flies so far each fall. On its zigzag journey southward, this warbler often covers more than 6,000 miles from Alaska to New England, then over the seas to South America.

Jonathan Blair (all)

On a radar screen, two million night-migrating songbirds show up as moving green dots. Researchers use this radar at the airport in Greenville, South Carolina, to study how changing weather conditions affect migration. Radar data also reveal the approximate speed, altitudes, and number of migrants, including transoceanic travelers flying at 21,000 feet. Birds prefer to depart after passage of cold fronts, when winds help push them on their way. Most songbirds travel at night to avoid hungry predators. Waterfowl can fly by night or day.

Under the night sky of a planetarium, Indigo Buntings (left) quickly take their directional cues from the artificial stars. Researchers at Cornell University put these songbirds in cages with ink pads for floors. With the stars turned off (upper), a bird skitters aimlessly, making ink tracks all over the cage.

When shown the stars (lower), a bird moves confidently to the northeast, its normal course for spring migration. Like mariners, birds may steer by Polaris and the stars that cluster round it. But these avian travelers have other guides as well—sun, wind, magnetic fields, landmarks, and the movements of other birds.

Jonathan Blair (all)

made over water by small birds anywhere in the world. Most land birds prefer to remain just that—sticking to land on migration, the experienced members of the flocks making use of landmarks to guide them on their way. They seem to go to great lengths to avoid crossing large bodies of water. Their reluctance is readily apparent at prominent points of land that jut into the water, where flocks of birds begin to pile up on the fall migration.

Such a bottleneck occurs at Cape May, New Jersey. Birds flying south along the shore suddenly reach the tip of Cape May Point and discover they must fly over a broad stretch of Delaware Bay. Perhaps they fear being blown out to sea by a northwest wind. Sometimes thousands of birds, including strong fliers such as Sharp-shinned Hawks, mill about over the point, utterly frustrated at the prospect. Many of them, rather than attempt the crossing, turn and fly *north* for 30 to 50 miles to a point where the bay narrows and provides a more comfortable crossing.

One of the advantages of flight over land for songbirds is that when they grow weary or hungry, they are able to drop to earth and rest for a while. The vast stretches of urban areas along our coastlines, and even in the important river valleys inland, would seem to discourage these temporary stops, but small songbirds make good use of isolated plots of greenery. City bird watchers haunt parks, cemeteries, and even garbage dumps because they know migrants may be concentrated there in unusual numbers. Over a period of some years an enthusiastic birder has counted 102 species in the miniscule garden behind his brownstone house on New York City's densely crowded East Side.

Bird watchers on the west coast of the United States and Canada take advantage of a different aspect of bird behavior. Each year the birders' hotlines hum with the news that rare birds, generally referred to as vagrants, have appeared here and there along the coast. For the most part they belong to species that nest in the far north and usually fly east to the Atlantic coast. There they turn south to complete their migration. These vagrants are lost birds. They suffer from what ornithologists term mirror-image navigation. Their internal compasses are somehow awry, so that they fly in a direction opposite from that for which their species has been programmed by evolution.

The east coast, too, has its vagrants—mostly in fall—but by far the greater number of mirror-image birds are found along the Pacific shore. When they reach the coastline, they turn south. A few winter in southern California and Mexico. Others, when the coastline curves sharply eastward, undoubtedly continue flying south and perish at sea.

Open water is the greatest single hazard for migrating birds. Each fall the toll must run into the millions, compounded by birds that normally use ocean routes or are blown off course by high winds. Scientists tell of finding the feathers of small birds in the stomachs of deep-sea fish.

Many a sailor has his tale of exhausted birds expiring on the deck or clinging to a ship's rigging in foul weather. In the days before modern methods of slaughter decimated the sea mammals and other creatures, the broad backs of whales and turtles were said to provide emergency landing sites occasionally for winded birds at sea.

Many migrants are not so fortunate. Some are taken by predators, such as the Peregrine Falcon; others are killed by human hunters. A far greater number lose their lives in collisions with man-made structures. Biologists picked up 2,117 individuals of 37 species one September morning at the foot of a television tower in Eau Claire, Wisconsin.

For many years it was believed that migrant birds rigidly restricted themselves to four major north-south routes through North America. Biologists designated them as the Atlantic, Mississippi, Central, and Pacific flyways. They now recognize that the flyway concept was an oversimplification of a movement that takes place across a broad front, but it has proved useful to federal officials in establishing management regions for migrating waterfowl.

Each species has evolved its own patterns of migration. A clue to this development comes from recent studies of shorebirds departing from their breeding grounds in the far north. One characteristic of this order is that adults leave the breeding territory before their young, even while food supplies abound. The early departure is a possible advantage to the older birds that arrive on the feeding grounds first and have first choice of the food. The younger ones that arrive later are at a great disadvantage because less food remains for them.

But what triggers the departure itself? Researchers closely followed the feeding habits of three migrant shorebird species—Short-billed Dowitchers, Sanderlings, and Semipalmated Sandpipers—on marshes and intertidal flats in Massachusetts from July through September. The Short-billed Dowitchers fed on bamboo worms, amphipods, and small clams, while the Sanderlings and Semipalmated Sandpipers preyed mainly on little shrimp. By the middle of September these tiny marine organisms on which the shorebirds fed had considerably decreased in numbers.

Shorebirds arriving late in the summer at this staging area found the flats and marshes well picked over. They might have a difficult time building up energy for the arduous flight ahead. Because the latecomers' chances of survival are diminished, natural selection favors the early birds. Those birds reaching the feeding grounds early are the winners in the battle for survival and, in an evolutionary sense, shape their species' migratory patterns.

Shorebirds generally migrate by day. Although observations of radar screens have determined their flight speed to be about 45 miles per hour (more than one-third faster than that of small songbirds), shorebirds often seem not to be in any great hurry. Fall migration tends to be more leisurely than that in spring, when birds are intent on arriving early at their destination to stake out territories and find mates.

Yet leisure is hardly the word that comes to mind when we observe another phase of the fall migration. The sight of thousands of hawks streaming south along inland ridges has stimulated highly different emotions among Americans ever since colonial times. The Europeans who settled this continent frequently brought with them a gamekeeper's attitude toward the large birds of prey. Hawks were vermin, to be killed on sight. Unfortunately, the hawks' distinctive migratory course proved to be the single greatest cause of their destruction.

Shooting migrant hawks was, until very recently, a popular fall pastime throughout the eastern and midwestern United States. Many species of hawks, including Broadwings, Redtails, and Sharpshins, traditionally migrated in flocks. Prime conditions for a large flight are created by a strong cold front and winds out of the south or northwest. These winds, striking the sides of hills and mountains, are deflected and provide updrafts on which hawks soar southward.

Hunters, taking advantage of this, stationed themselves at good observation points along the ridges. Two of the most infamous shooting places were Hawk Mountain, a spur of the Kittatinny Ridge in the Appalachians near Reading, Pennsylvania, and Hawk Ridge, within the city limits of Duluth, Minnesota. Up to 300 hawks of eight to ten species were shot from the sky at these mountain overlooks during an average day's "varmint shoot."

All this has changed in recent decades. Largely through the efforts of Rosalie Edge, one of the most flamboyant and effective figures in conservation history, and Maurice Broun, the biologist who doubled as a game warden for years of hazardous duty, Hawk Mountain became a sanctuary in 1934 for the migrant birds of prey. Duluth's Hawk Ridge Nature Reserve, founded in 1972 by the Duluth Audubon Society, rivals the Pennsylvania sanctuary as a vantage point from which to view the great autumn flights today. But both reserves are more than simply sites for a gathering of bird watchers on windy autumn days; they are reminders that the strict protection of any bird's breeding and wintering grounds may not be sufficient if the bird remains vulnerable on its migration.

Hawk migrations are not nearly so concentrated in the far west, where birds of prey tend to fly south over a wide front. The Broadwing's counterpart as a flocking species in the west is the Swainson's Hawk, which seems to have decreased in recent years. Yet this species may still be seen in impressive numbers as the southbound flocks reach the narrowing landmass of Central America. Observers counted almost 300,000 Swainson's Hawks flying over Panama City during October and November 1973, and more than 200,000 in the autumn of 1976.

The Swainson's Hawk is one of the Americas' most remarkable migrants, supporting the recent contention that neither north nor south can rightfully claim such species as its own. This hawk spends four months of every year on the North American plains, four months on the pampas of Argentina, and four months making its way from one region to the other. Despite its long migrations, the Swainson's Hawk apparently does not build up deposits of fat in preparation for its departure. Moreover, it fasts for much of the time en route, only occasionally pausing to feed on the insects it finds along the way. This astonishing conduct can be attributed to its mechanics of flight. Small, short-winged birds expend tremendous amounts of energy on migration because they have to flap their wings continuously to keep aloft. But the Swainson's Hawk conserves its strength: It soars with motionless wings on hot air bubbles, called thermals, which ascend from the valleys it follows south.

Alexander Skutch, a naturalist who has watched these migrants in Costa Rica, describes their flight as "bartering altitude for distance." He saw them alternately circle into the sky on a thermal updraft, glide forward for a time on motionless wings, then break away to "enter the bottom of the next feathered whirlpool" and soar to new heights.

The hawks even glide up the front of advancing storms and pass over them at 20,000 feet or more. Most of the birds continue all the way to Argentina, where they will find a ready source of food in wandering flights of locusts.

We can see, and wonder at, the teeming flocks of hawks and shorebirds, but what of the small songbirds that fly by night? When migrating over land, they come to earth at dawn, ready to feed and rest all day until darkness and a favoring wind send them on their way once more. One of these small migrants, the Blackpoll Warbler, has adopted a complex route over thousands of miles of land and water.

In the distant past the Blackpoll probably nested only in the evergreen forests of eastern North America. Slowly it extended its breeding range far into northwestern Canada and Alaska. Now the members of this northwestern segment of the population, instead of flying directly south, retrace every fall on migration the path over which the species originally expanded its range.

It is no coincidence that this long-range flier has evolved longer, more powerful wings than most other warblers. As the days grow shorter in late summer, the Blackpoll Warblers leave the forests of the northwest and fly toward the southeast, through the Great Lakes region to the Maritime Provinces and the northeastern United States. Then they launch themselves out over the Atlantic and Caribbean.

For three or four days these one-ounce packets of flesh and feathers (they could be mailed to any point in the United States or Canada for the price of a first-class postage stamp) are at the mercy of the sea. It is testament to their adaptability that these diminutive birds, whose home is alternately the boreal forests of Canada and the tropical woodlands of Brazil, live through these wind-driven hours over the ocean, at one with the terns and storm petrels.

Perhaps, on that fateful October day in 1492, Blackpolls were among the migrant flocks over the Caribbean Sea that Christopher Columbus pointed out to his faint-hearted crew as harbingers of an approaching landfall. The Admiral of the Ocean Sea could not have guessed that those tiny navigators in the sky were still hundreds of miles from a destination many of them, like himself, had never seen before.

Sandpipers cruise by the shore of James Bay, Ontario (right), where they fatten during a stopover on their journeys to Central and South America. Building fat reserves to fuel flight, some birds double their weight in three weeks by feasting on mollusks and insects. In a single year the Red Knot, a type of sandpiper, migrates 20,000 miles between the Arctic and Tierra del Fuego at South America's tip.

To study the migratory habits of the Red Knot, Canadian scientists dyed birds captured at James Bay with an orange stain (below) for later identification. In an experiment involving 32 marked birds, three of them (including the one shown opposite below) were found in Suriname, almost 4,000 miles away in South America.

Jonathan Blair (all)

Lured back to its ancestral summer home, the Atlantic Puffin (opposite) reappears on the coast of Maine. A century ago, hunters seeking meat and feathers eliminated the birds in the region. With help from the National Audubon Society, puffin chicks from Newfoundland—a thousand miles away—are now brought "home," where they are snugged down in their nesting burrows (right) amid the rocks.

When the chicks are about 50 days old, they flutter into the ocean to spend their first two years at sea. In June of their third year, many return to their adopted island to spend the summer. On such a visit one Egg Rock adoptee with a "Class of '75" leg band (below) stands with three decoys that help attract other puffins to the island.

OVERLEAF: Swirling and white as a snowstorm, a flock of Snow Geese takes wing after feeding on a plowed grainfield near Tule Lake, California, their winter home. These geese arrive each fall from Siberia and the Canadian Arctic. Other arctic-born Snow Geese may fly more than 2,000 miles nonstop to winter as far south as Mexico.

Jonathan Blair (also opposite). Below: Stephen Kress, Cornell University. Overleaf: Art Wolfe

187

The Enduring Challenge

By Franklin Russell

ithin the rock walls of a Baffin Island fjord, a single snowflake, gossamer fine, drifts from a leaden sky and gently falls into itself in the mirrored waters. A small flock of male Common Eiders floats motionless in the middle of the fjord as if painted in place in a still landscape of grays, browns, and steely blues. At the edge of a precipice stands an unblinking Snowy Owl.

The fall of the snowflake is a sign of one season seeking to overcome another. In this month, late September, the North American winter has begun. But it has not yet achieved enough authority to take control.

The waiting owl, a lustrous and imperial figure in his speckled white plumage, is looking south with large yellow eyes. Soon he must fly into that sunward unknown, for here in the Arctic his main food supply of lemmings has dwindled drastically in one of the rodents' cyclical population crashes. The owl has no choice but to migrate, to intrude deeper into a continent where hundreds of species of birds are already wintering over—migrants and residents, shorebirds and waterfowl, desert dwellers and woodland foragers, beach prowlers and prairie wanderers, seed eaters and meat hunters—and there find food in strange new surroundings.

Tundra born, the owl has never seen a tree. Yet he will have to accustom himself to forests, lakes, rivers, then farms, towns, cities. He will be harassed by birds flocked to drive him away. He will be seen flaring away from airplane landing lights, a limp rodent dangling from

A Short-eared Owl finds shelter amid cedars in upstate New York. By Michael Jacob Hopiak.

his talons. Danger will haunt him even in the seemingly familiar: He can be struck by an airplane if he eats his prey on the tundra-like expanse of the airport tarmac.

As with the owl, so with most birds: Winter is the challenge of finding food amid high risk and sometimes bizarre dangers. Thousands of birds may die in a few hours during an ice storm in Kansas or a sudden freeze in Minnesota. But·there is actually no true shortage of food at any time, only changes in where it is available. And so, by feats of competition, cooperation, and adaptation, North America's birds will place themselves in the coming months over many millions of square miles of the earth's surface, exactly where the right food is available at the right time.

The drama-to-come involves a stupendous cast. At summer's end the United States and Canada hold some twenty billion birds, and the coming winter will affect nearly every one of them. Perhaps eight billion will migrate beyond the southern borders of the United States. And one out of three of these travelers will die before spring.

The birds must move, shift their behavior patterns, change in many ways, to find the food. It is hidden by snow, ice, water, mud, leaves, sand, earth, bark. It is created seasonally as caterpillars swarm in Texas, locusts multiply in Patagonia, trees go to seed in Maine, crustaceans proliferate in New England foreshores and off California beaches. It must be apportioned among the many birds seeking it at the same time.

*T*he quest for food, and for the places where food is to be found, gives the season its vitality—its prodigies of travel, nuances of behavior, astonishing mixes of species in the common act of discovery that is winter. The owl may fly 4,000 miles in its ongoing search for food. Shorebirds can climb to 20,000 feet on their migration flights to find secure feeding places. The Greater Shearwater flies so low over the ocean that it often cuts the waves with its wing tips. But it can travel nonstop from Massachusetts to the Tristan da Cunha Islands, between the tips of Africa and South America, to fish for its winter food.

Winter survival is a drama of evolution responding to environment. Each species of bird, from eighth-of-an-ounce hummingbirds to 30-pound Trumpeter Swans, has its own kit of survival capabilities.

All birds, like all mammals, have their vital organs encased in a protective shell, which maintains an acceptable temperature for the organs. In birds this insulating shell consists of feathers, skin, legs, and feet. Birds that winter in cold regions have evolved specialized insulation and respiratory systems, which serve two vital purposes: to keep the cold out and to enable the organs to function as a hot core. The legs of the Willow Ptarmigan and Snowy Owls are covered with feathers to reduce heat loss. Many birds, such as the redpolls of Alaska, have more feathers in winter than in summer; their feathers weigh 31 percent more in November than in July. The eiders may plunge as deep as 100 feet to find shellfish in the sea, even when the water temperature is 29°F.

Their heartbeats pulse at 200 a minute but can comfortably rise to 400 as they fly into a stiff sea breeze.

Eiders are encased in a sheath of several thousand feathers, all of which are being changed in the molt they are undergoing in the fjord. The molt has made them flightless for about three weeks while new winter feathers grow into place. Their down feathers—those closest to the skin—have the best insulating properties of any bird's, enabling the eiders to keep warm all winter, even when temperatures plunge to 50°F below zero. With the return of flight power, when their long primary wing feathers have grown out to full length, the eiders will fly directly to their wintering grounds along the coast of Newfoundland, about 2,000 miles south of the fjord. There, as they fly in single file between the waves, the ducks return to a place they know, a place of plentiful food where shellfish beds lie just offshore.

The lone Snowy Owl and the flocked eiders symbolize two ways of handling the challenge of winter. Beyond them lie countless variations of aloneness and togetherness, of moving and standing fast, which match the birds with amazing exactness to the placement of food. Young Arctic Terns that hatched in the tundra country of the Snowy Owl's home territory feed on crustaceans in Antarctica, more than 12,000 miles away. Geese that bred in Saskatchewan and Manitoba eat cornfield gleanings in Missouri, aquatic plants in Oklahoma, ricefield leavings in Texas—and wheat, corn, and soybeans planted for them at wildlife refuges. Kingbirds that nested in North America not only migrate but also make a radical change in diet, switching from flying insects to mistletoe berries and tree fruits in Central and South America.

Chickadees that bred in the northern states stay close to home in winter, poking into bark crannies for cocoons and insect eggs, searching for seeds in evergreen cones and suburban feeders. Gathering in small flocks, the birds scout out several favorite foraging spots in a loosely defined territory. A feeding flock of these nervously active little birds will be likely to frequent the same thicket, wood, or hedgerow throughout the winter as they make their rounds in small groups. With them may be titmice, nuthatches, Brown Creepers, and a woodpecker or two, all members of the flock, yet usually lagging behind the chickadees and titmice that seem to set the pace with their more active searching behavior. The most agile are the chickadees; when snow blankets the evergreens, they continue to feed, hanging upside down to rummage for seeds and dormant insects on the undersides of the branches.

Most waterfowl will move no farther south than they are forced to by ice or shortages of food. They collect in huge congregations—millions at the Klamath Basin National Wildlife Refuges on the Oregon-California border, millions in the southern California irrigation system of dams, ponds, levees, and the artificially created Salton Sea. Millions more waterfowl will crisscross the nation's midsection, feeding by the dams of the U. S. Army Corps of Engineers, on ponds, rivers, and lakes, in farmers' fields of wheat, corn, and rice. Hundreds of thousands of waterfowl will be found on the estuaries, islands, and inlets of Chesapeake Bay and on the shores of the Carolinas and Georgia.

Other birds may fly awesome distances to find places where their principal food is plentiful. Sanderlings, cardinal-size shorebirds, prey on sand crabs found only on unfrozen beaches. So the Sanderlings stream out of the northlands each fall in search of this crab. Most of the birds fly from northern Canada to Peru and Chile, pausing to spell themselves on beaches along the way. Long, pointed wings speed them southward at 40 to 50 miles an hour along unerring lines of navigation. Speed lets them feed at places scores of miles apart. Their aerial agility is like the flick of an eyelid, 10,000 birds turning instantaneously to foil the waiting Merlins, the harrying hawks, the deadly Peregrines.

Eventually a group of Sanderlings reaches the mouth of the Tambo River in Peru, a lush marsh country set against a desert hinterland. The flight from the Arctic has taken a hundred hours.

Once settled, some of the Sanderlings split off from the flock to stake out and defend individual feeding territories. But, like the owl, they must respond to the actions of other creatures. When a falcon appears, it soon learns that the hunting is best among these loners. So the Sanderlings abandon their territories and rejoin the flock. The falcon must then hunt the grouped birds. It approaches the flock, which rises into the air as one huge mass, a churning column of Sanderlings turning one way, then another, flashing in the sun. The falcon, confounded, departs.

A 20-pound Wild Turkey in Oklahoma migrates 3 miles from the bed of the Canadian River to reach a grove of pecans. A Rufous Hummingbird flies 2,600 miles from a mountain meadow in Idaho to the slopes of twin volcanoes in Mexico, where it feeds on insects and awaits the opening of cup-shaped flowers that soon bloom there in profusion. Gulls seem to do anything that works: migrate when necessary, fly from shore to inland, from inland to shore. Some Heermann's Gulls and Elegant Terns migrate *north* in winter. Much depends on where the food is located, on where the storms are blowing, and perhaps on mysteries not understood by man.

Those jewels of the summer American woodlands, the wood warblers, nearly all leave their North American haunts and settle in jungles, mountains, cloud forests, islands, estuaries, and desert fringes from Mexico through the Caribbean to northern Bolivia. Some warbler species flock, some are solitary, some join the flocks of other birds; their behavior is as varied in winter as their colors are brilliant in summer. The great meat-hunters, those terrors of almost all the other birds—the eagles, falcons, hawks, and owls—are as various in their handling of winter as the birds and insects and rodents on which they prey. One Peregrine Falcon may remain in a bay in Washington, eating Dunlins. Another may travel 8,500 miles to southern Patagonia and prey on North American shorebirds there. Great Horned Owls stay in place. In some years only a small percentage of Snowy Owls come south; in other years most of the entire arctic population makes the trek.

The Snowy Owl perched on a Baffin Island precipice swivels his round head for a last look at the eiders in the fjord. Then his wings stretch out to a five-foot span and lift him from the cliff top. Day after day they carry him noiselessly southward.

He meets other northern birds intent on their own search for food. Snow Buntings, which occasionally become a meal for the owl, fall like snowflakes among grasses bowed under a clinging snow. Redpolls— small northern finches—punctuate the silence with their chirring calls.

Somewhere east of Hudson Bay the owl sights his first trees, a straggle of spruces climbing a rocky slope. He must go down among those trees, and cross hundreds of miles of uninterrupted forest if need be, for the unknown ahead of him is less forbidding than the hunger behind. Birds he has never seen before may now become food for the owl, a rodent hunter far from his native tundra.

The thickening forests roll beneath the owl's wings. He has no experience or special fitness for hunting here. But he hunts as well by night as by day, for in his native Arctic regions both daylight and darkness can last for months.

In fading twilight he glides into a meadow and perches on a rock. Sensitive ears set well apart in a broad skull pinpoint the rustlings of a mouse in the grass nearby. His head swivels on his supple neck, aiming eyes so huge they cannot move. An owl's eyes must not only render the needle-sharp images a hunting bird needs, but must do it in extremely low light. This requires enormous eyeballs—so enormous they must be supported by tubes of bone that protrude from the skull like stubby binoculars. Most birds have large eyes; in some, including the owls, the eyeballs take up more skull space than the brain. But some crows, gulls, cuckoos, and many other birds can move their eyes in varying degrees. The owl's are locked immovably in place.

The Snowy Owl's lenses gather in the faint images as he launches himself off the rock and swoops toward the mouse. His vision is superb at a distance but relatively poor up close, so at the last moment his eyelids wink shut to protect the eyes that he no longer needs to complete the kill. His talons strike and sink deep. Next morning a wisp of blood-tinged fur will litter the rock; another day, and a wad of bones and fur will pock the snow in a forest clearing as the owl coughs up a pellet of parts he cannot digest.

The Snowy Owl can survive for days without food. His chunky body is sheathed in fat, which he can use instead of food for energy. His feathers are so dense that he is nearly impervious to that great killer of birds: cold wind. His wings are muffled with soft feathers that make his flight as silent as starlight.

The drifting, silent passage of the owl is like the advance of winter itself, subtle yet pervasive. The creatures that he meets are readying themselves for the onset of winter's dangers. Willow Ptarmigan burst into the air from a slope in the rolling hills of interior Labrador. They bred prolifically in the summer, but the local supply of willow and alder buds is already disappearing under the winter's early snows and soon will not be available to feed these new populations. So the birds fly off in

Dressed for two seasons, a male Willow Ptarmigan (opposite) perches in a willow in Alaska's Denali National Park. In the middle of his spring molt, he wears in May both the reddish brown of summer and the snowy white of winter.

A few weeks earlier all but his black tail feathers were white; a few weeks more and his mottled browns will reach from head to tail and will hide him amid tundra and thicket. Some white stays year round. Four Willow Ptarmigan in Denali (below) show white highlights in the plumage of August.

Jen and Des Bartlett. Opposite: Rick McIntyre

Two silent snowballs in a drifted Canadian thicket suddenly come to life as one of them nibbles off a willow bud. In their winter plumage Willow Ptarmigan show black only on bills, eyes, and outer tail feathers. Their white-on-white camouflage helps to hide them in a world of snow and ice; the black remaining in their tails may serve as "flags" to help keep winter flocks together in flight.

The snow that blankets the tundra drives these small arctic grouse into sheltered valleys and forest edges, where they forage on buds and twigs of alder and willow. But the snow is both bane and gift. Though it hides the tundra plants and berries that fattened the birds all summer, it gives them on winter nights a shelter from chilly winds and predators, a haven such as the open tundra rarely provides. Straight into the snowbanks the hardy ptarmigan fly, leaving no trail of footprints for a predator to follow. Straight out again they fly in the morning, after a night's rest in warmth and safety.

George W. Calef

Here the birds coexist in a mosaic of food hunting that is supremely specialized, much more so than in North America. Some birds cannot feed until army ants march and scare up food for them.

Into that tight mosaic the North American migrants must somehow fit. As the army ants forage across the forest floor, several migrant birds—Wood Thrushes, Kentucky Warblers, Veeries—join the resident woodcreepers and antbirds that feed on the harvest of insects and spiders the ants flush. But the resident birds crowd toward the swarm's leading edge, where the hunting is best; any migrant that tries to feed among them is promptly and easily chased away. Only by feeding on the fringes can the migrants share in the feast.

Eastern Kingbirds eat flying insects as the birds migrate down through Central America. But in Panama heavy seasonal rains sometimes ground all the insects. The birds turn to eating fruit, which is fast-fattening food. When they reach Amazonia, this change of habit should result in their being driven from the fruit crops by the resident birds. And indeed, the residents attack them repeatedly. But there are so many kingbirds that the residents cannot stop the huge flocks from feeding.

A Canada Warbler reaching Colombia's Anchicayá Valley finds 300 species of resident birds claiming almost every inch of space. But the warbler's habit of plucking insects from the undersides of leaves near the ground is shared by few of the resident birds and is thus an advantage because insects are now sheltering there from the heavy rains. By not competing directly, the warbler can coexist in the territories of others.

Some birds fit in by joining flocks of residents, as do many vireos, tanagers, and warblers, and so enjoy the advantage of scores of experienced eyes watching for enemies in the tropical forest. A Blackburnian Warbler arriving in the Anchicayá attaches itself to a roving band of residents of different species, one Blackburnian to a flock. When "outsider" Blackburnians attempt to join such a band, they are challenged by the Blackburnian "owner." Yet, within the flock, the Blackburnian member is lowest in the pecking order.

So many insects are competing for a place in the jungle—probably millions of species, including 150 species of mosquitoes in the Anchicayá alone—that deception and concealment have been brought to high arts. The Prothonotary Warbler from South Carolina prowls a mangrove jungle in Venezuela and pecks at a glistening bead of water on a leaf. The leaf flies away. Insects that masquerade as leaves come in hundreds of varieties.

The resident birds are not so easily fooled. A nomadic Kentucky Warbler, foraging in the low growth of a Central American forest, ignores a bird dropping on the branch at its feet. A resident Streak-chested Antpitta—a tailless ground dweller that resembles a long-legged thrush—snaps it up, knowing that it is a caterpillar in disguise.

The unseen challenge of winter for many birds, in both North and

South America, hinges on the fact that so many of them fail to win territories. They must become "floaters," birds that drift like tiny ghosts in winter-long search for food wherever it can be found. They do not know the territories they must enter daily. Most are probably young birds from North America, the spillover from a massive overproduction of creatures that will be ground up in the ecological mills of tropical America. When spruce budworms attack New England conifers, young Bay-breasted Warblers of the region may be six times more abundant there than in a normal year. Yet adult numbers remain steady, for many of the youngsters will die during migration and many others will perish as floaters in the tropics.

North America knows its floaters too, and the Snowy Owl is one of them. He might never have moved from his nesting area if the lemmings had remained plentiful and accessible in the snow.

Now he drifts southwestward in quest of winter food. In Michigan he comes upon a vale of plenty. Westerly winds blowing across Lake Michigan have picked up some of the summer warmth stored in the deep lake and created a 5-degree-warmer "shadow" on lands to leeward. There the field mice flourish under a thin covering of snow. But a female Snowy Owl—another floater forced down from the Arctic by the scarcity of food—is already hunting there. She is larger than the male, and so she attacks him and drives him out.

Eventually the Snowy Owl wanders southward, stopping to hunt along river bottoms of Indiana and Ohio, toward the Mississippi River. Now he collides with flock after flock of crows, blackbirds, robins, and other birds. Sometimes a flock of crows harasses him, swooping and scolding as he stops to rest or hunt in daylight. He has no time to learn that an owl in southern regions can hunt more comfortably at night.

The flock offers the smaller birds safety in numbers. But even some of the larger birds congregate in winter, for the flock is a superb device for dealing with stress and danger. The Snowy Owl is no real threat to Canada Geese, yet when he approaches a large gathering of them in Oklahoma, nonfeeding geese acting as sentries react to the intrusion and honk an alarm. Thousands of geese rise with an intimidating thunder of wings. The owl turns away.

The flock also increases the chances of finding food. Different species of sparrows flock together in the Mojave and Sonoran Deserts, and throughout the southwest, to form more efficient groups of seed gatherers. In the Mojave the Brewer's Sparrows and Chipping Sparrows lead the flock, followed closely by the Blackthroats. White-crowned and Black-chinned Sparrows come next, then House Finches, a trail of Dark-eyed Juncos, and finally a Green-tailed Towhee as a tailpiece. Each species has a slightly different foraging behavior. Some hunt for seeds high in the bushes, some feed in the lower branches, some rummage among the herbs and grasses on the ground. The flock leaders move quickly through an area—at about a human's walking pace—and thus see less, leaving some food for birds that follow more slowly and observe more closely. As each bird influences the movements of the others, the flock is led back and forth across the desert (Continued on page 214)

A gathering of eagles brings hundreds of the stately raptors to the Klamath Basin that straddles the Oregon-California border. Drawn by the millions of waterfowl that spend the winter in the basin's six refuges, the Bald Eagles here muster their greatest concentration in the contiguous United States.

Swooping low, a lone eagle may flush a squadron of ducks, then seize any that lag behind. A goose is too big for an eagle to kill and drag from the water; most goose kills are of sick or dead birds already stranded on land or ice. Even so, the prize is not easily won; often it must be defended as other eagles move in to pirate the kill. One strides to a slain Snow Goose (right) and blusters its owner aside (below). Another eagle stands over another goose (opposite) and screams a warning to any eagle nearby.

Tupper Ansel Blake (all)

206

Erwin and Peggy Bauer. Right: Michael S. Quinton

208

A Clark's Nutcracker in a Wyoming forest finds horns of plenty amid the scarcity of winter. A bighorn ram has died—exhausted, perhaps, by the autumn rut, then felled by a severe winter and devoured by coyotes. To the nutcracker the upturned skull proffers the leftovers. Carrion often varies the bird's main fare of evergreen seeds.

Another bighorn—this one a healthy Montana lamb—lets a Black-billed Magpie check its scalp for ticks (below). Winter offers few such morsels, but the magpie's varied diet includes ample alternatives: small rodents, grain, even carrion along the roadsides.

Eastern Bluebirds cope with the cold of a Maryland winter. On a fence post a male (opposite) puffs up his feathers for better insulation on a bleak day in February. When night falls, he will roost in the hollowed post where he and his mate reared their summer brood. He may have company; on bitter cold nights a dozen birds or more may crowd in to share their own body heat.

To document this crowding behavior, the photographer fitted a nesting hollow with a lid, then removed it at night to find 13 bluebirds huddled inside (below). One night the hollow held 16—including 2 bluebirds that had died, apparently of suffocation.

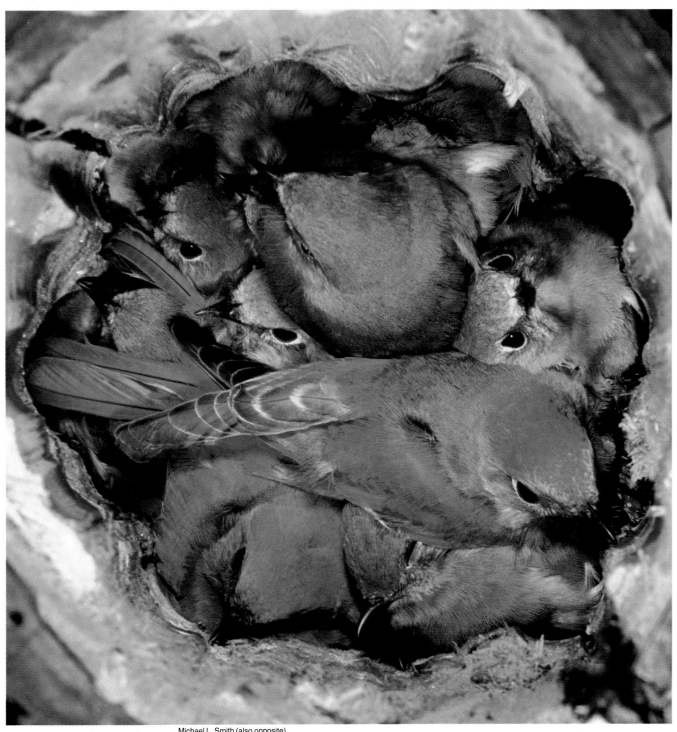

Michael L. Smith (also opposite)

Like spokes of a wheel, a covey of bobwhites settles down for a winter's night under the shelter of a juniper in Missouri. Their bodies press together for warmth; their heads aim outward for an unobstructed—and explosive—getaway if danger threatens. Favorite roosting spots, usually in sheltered areas, bear a telltale circle of droppings at the center.

Falling snow often covers the birds with an insulating blanket. But if the snow turns to freezing rain, it may crust over and form a prison.

About a dozen bobwhites of all ages and both sexes make up a covey, the males with white eye lines and throats, the females with buff. In spring the birds disperse to pair off and rear their young. Then the coveys form again, roosting in the round for safety if not for warmth.

Glenn D. Chambers

212

in a strikingly accurate exploitation of the available food. So thorough is the harvest that the flock promptly detours when it comes to an area it has already covered, since almost no food remains there. Competition within the flock may be intense, but it is controlled by the order of dominance, or hierarchy—the pecking order.

The Snowy Owl meanders into central Tennessee. The white plumage that made him nearly invisible in snowfields farther north now reveals him starkly in the bluegrass pastures. The crows can spot him more easily, and they move in to mob him. He suddenly buys a respite by flipping on his back and catching one of the crows. He eats it while the others scream at him from the trees. Thus the hunter and the hunted dance their gavotte of chase and flight, attack and evasion.

Slowly the winter wears on and the food resources dwindle. It is now mid-February. Blue Jays and White-breasted Nuthatches have eased the search for winter food by storing their gleanings in knothole and bark cranny for use when supplies run low. The jay can be an absent-minded storekeeper, sometimes eating a cache it put away only minutes before, sometimes abandoning a cache to whatever opportunist may discover it months later. Mockingbirds have long since fenced off their feeding territories with song and ritualized face-off; they reinforce the boundaries with occasional bursts of melody even in the dead of winter.

Now many millions of birds wintering in North America face one of the season's severest challenges—an advance of bitterly cold air 2,000 miles wide, from Montana to Maine, a breeder of windstorms, blizzards, ice storms, heavy rains. The challenge had been to find food; now the storm front will make the little food that is left even harder to find.

Cold and scarcity: Together they can wipe out complete populations. Long cold spells in the 1970s all but obliterated the bluebirds in Illinois and Indiana.

Along the Iowa-Minnesota border, thousands of titmice perish during the first few nights of the freeze. Carolina Wrens, a predominantly southern species, used to overwinter here too; freezing weather in 1974 eliminated them from the area.

In northern Minnesota, crossbills are sleeping in the boughs of evergreens. They are highly cold resistant, but with a gale blowing the snow, windchill temperatures plummet to 90°F below zero for the more exposed birds. When roosting, the dominant birds secure places deepest in thickets. That leaves the least dominant birds closer to the wind. More exposed and with less fat reserves, they are the first to die on the coldest nights. The fat that helps to insulate them can now be used to generate warmth through a process called catabolism, the destructive part of metabolism in which the breakdown of fatty substances, triggered by hormones and muscular activity, releases energy in the form of heat. This is usually achieved easily enough during the day when the bird is moving. But at night catabolism needs a trigger.

So the birds start to shiver in their sleep. A muscle used in raising a wing and an opposing muscle used in lowering it begin to contract in rapid rhythm against each other; thus each is exercised while the wing remains unmoved. So also do opposing sets of muscles tug at each other

214

from head to tail, causing all of the body to quiver. This is catabolism at work, and body heat is boosted at once.

As long as the crossbills' fat stores hold out, the "burn" of fat will not deplete the rest of their body tissue. But when the fat is gone, the birds will begin drawing energy from their muscles and so start consuming that dynamic part of their bodies that gives them flight and permits their agile searches for conifer seeds. They will begin to weaken, then they will die. Meanwhile, millions of sleeping birds—cardinals, goldfinches, grosbeaks, and others—shiver against the fierce cold, their lives now turned upon how long their fat will last.

Alaskan chickadees, more accustomed to bitter cold, respond with another life-saving adjustment. They shorten their foraging days. Or in particularly harsh weather, they stay in their roosts. Flight not only burns energy reserves but lets cold reach into feathers disturbed by the beating of the wings. They also conserve precious energy at night when their body temperatures may drop from 104°F to 84°. They take in less food in a shorter hunting day, but they use their fat reserves at a lower rate and so have a better chance of outlasting the freeze.

The Sharp-tailed Grouse of the northern Plains states can no longer feed on the ground, so they take to the tops of the green ash and cottonwood trees to nip the buds there. In New Jersey, cardinals rouse from sleep later each morning of the cold spell as they seek to conserve their internal fat reserves. Bird feeders become vital to survival.

The freeze rolls into Florida and overwhelms a hundred thousand Tree Swallows. Thousands take to the air at once and fly up through the advancing wedge of cold air until they reach the warmer air displaced by it. Then they head out to sea toward the Bahamas, where their kind used to migrate in the ancient past. It is a two-hour flight from Florida. Swallows carry light fat loads, enough for a short migration, four hours' supply at the most. After struggling free of the clinging chill, then making the flight to the Bahamas, they will have about an hour's reserve energy upon arrival, enough to begin stocking up on insects at the island chain. But they leave thousands of their fellows behind, dead and dying, scattered across highway and lawn, city and swamp.

Shelter now becomes the major device of survival. Bobwhites pack together in long dead grasses or in thickets for protection from the elements and hunters. Pheasants die in Montana because they cannot burrow into snow like Snow Buntings and ptarmigan, which dive into snowbanks and sleep there safe and warm. But if a fast thaw or a blizzard forms an ice crust on the snow, the sleeping birds can be sealed in. Their haven becomes a tomb.

The lash of winds demands shelter. But shelter may represent only the narrowest of margins between survival and catastrophe. Off the North Atlantic coast, Dovekies have no shelter as they skim along the tops of the waves. Thus a prolonged windstorm can blow these little seabirds

away, forcing a long return flight when the winds subside. But when an easterly gale sweeps them toward shore, they struggle against it, for there is little food for them on land. If they lose, a "wreck" begins. Thousands of Dovekies stream away helplessly in the grip of the sea wind. They flop inland, too exhausted to fly back to the sea and food.

The crisis of winter is, for many birds, the final challenge. For the birds that die are those at the edges of their flocks, those that are low in the hierarchies, that have failed in their bids for territory, that are less able to store fat, to seek and find shelter, to migrate and return. The winter thus sends just the strongest and healthiest creatures to the next challenge, the competition to breed.

The Snowy Owl, now northward bound, drifts over Great Horned Owls that are already nesting in northern Maine woodlands. Arctic Terns in southern seas are also beginning their long return flights, now dressed in their breeding plumage and ready for the shores of the North Atlantic and the Snowy Owl's north. In eastern Argentina tens of thousands of shorebirds have sent scuds of tiny, dull-colored feathers drifting into estuarine reeds and scampering along beaches that are being emptied, day by day, as birds gather into larger flocks for migration. The Sanderlings have molted and are highly excited, awaiting their signal to move. The Swainson's Hawks in Patagonia have built up fat by feeding on grasshoppers made listless by the chill winds of the South American autumn. Thrushes in Bolivia have fed on caterpillars. The vireos of Ecuador have fattened on fruit.

Great walls of birds will rise into these southern skies very soon now, pointed toward a land loosening itself from the last grip of snow and ice. Warblers in Costa Rica, hummingbirds in Nicaragua, Peregrine Falcons in Mexico—no migrant can refuse to move, to disobey the call north.

The gonads of birds everywhere are swelling. The juices of spring flow despite the weather, which to the north may still be bleak, cold, even ice laden. The skies of the middle western states, southern California, the Sacramento Valley, are skeined with excited waterfowl. Sparrows in the Mojave Desert are singing and squabbling in their flocks, even as late snow dusts the creosote bushes on their hunting grounds.

The Snowy Owl has now reached the limit of trees at the 56th parallel as he heads past the southern shores of Hudson Bay. The incomparable expanses of tundra and rock stretch ahead thousands of miles beyond his sight. Few Snowies wander as far as he has. But now he is home again, a survivor—like most of his kind—of the lemming famine, the arduous flight south, the long trek north.

As he symbolized the southbound migrants, so now he belongs to a returning parade of survivors, birds that were best able to seize and hold territories, to store fat, to change diets, to keep warm, to stay, to move, to fit in with residents, to intimidate competitors, to keep in rhyme with the perpetuating poem of nature.

The owl disappears into a snowstorm. His silent flight, like the soundless fall of a billion snowflakes and the stirrings of millions of winter-weary birds, cannot be stopped now any more than spring can be turned back by the dying challenge of winter.

Indigo Buntings nibble grass seeds in a Mexican pasture. They benefit as trees are cut for farming—but most migrants suffer, since most need forest habitats for wintering over. Because migrants crowd remaining forests, clearing one acre in Mexico or in the Caribbean islands now does the harm of clearing five to eight in northeastern North America.

A change of diet helps the Broad-winged Hawk through the winter. Broadwings may not eat for a month or more during migration. Some winter in Panama; no longer hunting small mammals, birds, and reptiles by day, they feed mainly on katydids at dusk. Other Broadwings prey on reptiles. In Ecuador's mountains one perches with a frog as vultures circle.

It is spring in the Argentine pampas when Buff-breasted Sandpipers from North America arrive. The resident Southern Lapwings are now rearing their young. But the sandpiper feeds where the lapwing mates—in the short grasses. Clashes are common; here a lapwing swoops in a fierce attack on a sandpiper that foraged too close to the lapwing's chicks.

Migrant Tennessee Warblers in Panama battle over the nectar of combretum flowers. The dominant birds win the right to feed first and soon become "war painted," their faces stained by the brilliant red pollen. Thus marked, the bird at right advertises his high status in the pecking order. Now they waste no energy in fighting; the lesser bird quickly defers.

Paintings by John Gurche

217

A crown of snow and a garland of bittersweet adorn a robin's nest in Illinois (opposite) as winter undoes the skillful craftsmanship of spring. The female built the nest; the male helped by supplying her with mud and grasses. If their construction survives the winter, they may build a new nest atop the old one next spring.

Spring's imperatives matter little in winter. Far from the territories they defended, migrant robins that would have routed each other as intruders now share a birdbath (below) on a Florida lawn.

Robert E. Pelham, Photo Researchers. Opposite: Lynn M. Stone

Cardinals (right) at a feeder in Ohio, a male Evening Grosbeak (below) at another in New Jersey—such are the rewards to humans whose offerings of seeds help ease the rigors of winter. Only a century ago the Evening Grosbeak was a western bird and the cardinal a resident of the south; now both are common in the northeastern *states as well. Feeders such as these may have helped both species gain a foothold. Each relishes sunflower seeds— and shells them neatly with a stout nutcracker bill.*

Laura Riley. Right: Dave Maslowski

220

The Hand of Man

By George Laycock

Billions of them once filled the American skies, blotting out the sun for hours. Then men and boys attacked the Passenger Pigeons with nets, guns, and clubs, and sent barrels of their carcasses to eastern markets. Meanwhile, farmers and timbermen destroyed the beech and oak forests where the wild pigeons nested and fed. By 1914 they had become the rarest birds in the world.

Like the pigeons, all of North America's birds once lived in a wilderness as wide as the continent, a region of fertile lands blanketed by deep green forests, broad sunlit prairies, and shimmering ponds and marshes. Mountain peaks reached into clear air while streams carried clean water down the slopes to the large rivers and the oceans.

Following the arrival of Europeans, however, this verdant land would have to support millions more humans than the scattered bands of native people who had lived here in simple harmony with their environment. Forests, prairies, and wetlands were in the way, and people would eventually replace these habitats with towns, cities, highways, shopping centers, reservoirs, and chemically treated land.

Through all the seasons, and wherever birds fly or nest, they must now share this transformed and crowded world with people, and we have only to look from the windows of our homes to see this. Beyond our yards there were once woods, wild flowers, brush, and grass from which came the liquid notes of meadowlarks, thrashers, towhees, and bluebirds. But subdivisions have spread over the land, and wild acres where the birds

A lone Whooping Crane climbs skyward. By Entheos.

lived are now neatly carved into uniform plots of short green grass surrounding modern homes. Beyond the suburbs lie the broad fields of grain and our carefully managed grasslands and forests.

By human standards our farming and building activities are desirable. But the chemicals and machines that keep the land productive for people often render it unfit for meadowlarks and bluebirds.

We leave unintended hazards in our wake. Birds crash into our windows and are killed on our highways; they become entangled in our fishing lines and caught in our oil spills. Birds have even been brought down by flying golf balls. Our radio and television towers, and the wires that hold them in place, kill an estimated one million birds a year. Birds that evolved in clear skies must now travel in the half-light of smoggy days and neon nights, and there is no tool for measuring the stress that these changes inflict on them.

Most destructive of all are the massive changes we make in habitats, with little thought given to the effects on wildlife. The hardwood forests were opened with ax and fire, the wind-rippled prairie grasses buried by the plow. To the pothole country of the northern prairies, where a world of half land, half water once provided a wild refuge for noisy crowds of waterfowl, there came what the famed naturalist Aldo Leopold called "an epidemic of ditch-digging and land-booming." In the lower 48 states our draining, ditching, and leveling eliminated more than half of the nation's original 215 million acres of marshes, ponds, and sloughs, where ducks, herons, cranes, and other birds once raised their young. Each year we drain nearly half a million acres of wetlands and put them to human use.

New developments in farming since World War II have replaced smaller family-size farms with giant agribusiness corporations. These big farms and their broad fields of single crops leave less food and cover for wildlife. The brushy fencerows and odd patches of cover vanish. A 1980 study in four midwestern states revealed that the number of bobwhites—quail that live in roadside hedges and overgrown fields—had fallen 50 percent in 20 years. The 1970s brought a bustling foreign demand for more food and fiber, and American farmers responded by putting another 50 million acres of once idle land into crop production.

Even in the wildest remaining corners of our continent, birds cannot escape human impact. The air and water carry foreign substances. Acid rain, created by our burning of fossil fuels, falls on the most remote wilderness, killing small organisms that feed fish—or destroying outright the fish that once supported herons, loons, and kingfishers. Parks are filled with people who add an unnatural element. The sounds of our voices, machines, pets, and music leave the wild birds no memories of the wilderness quiet they once knew.

Wildlife must also contend with foreign species that people brought to North America. Searching for birds that would improve hunting, or simply attempting to recapture the nostalgic memories of distant homelands, people turned loose hundreds of these imports.

Most imported birds have failed, but House Sparrows, starlings, and pigeons are irascible exceptions that quickly muscled their way into native wildlife communities and became permanent American residents.

After starlings were released in New York City's Central Park in 1890, the highly adaptable birds became an instant success: The first starling nest in America was discovered that same summer beneath the eaves of the American Museum of Natural History. From this and other seedings, starlings advanced across the country, boldly taking nest sites from bluebirds, flickers, and other birds that nest in cavities.

Even the beautiful Ring-necked Pheasant, brought to America from the Old World, became the enemy of native birds. Prairie chickens, already disappearing from mid-America's vanishing grasslands, were further harassed when aggressive cock pheasants drove them from their courting grounds and hen pheasants laid eggs in prairie chicken nests.

Any exotic bird or animal can inflict stress on the native birds. Packs of wild-running dogs kill or harass Wild Turkeys, grouse, and other birds that nest on the ground. Introduced goats have destroyed vegetation on San Clemente Island off the southern California coast, bringing the local Sage Sparrows near extinction.

Pressures mount. Those birds unable to adapt disappear silently from one area after the other until they are gone everywhere.

Amid the crowds of people at the Cincinnati Zoo stands a small, quaint stone building with a red tile roof. Three-quarters of a century ago this was the final home of what had become the world's rarest bird. Her name was Martha, and as far as anyone knew, she was the very last of the multitudes of Passenger Pigeons that once swept across the skies. When Martha died in 1914, she carried with her the last genes of her kind, a wild heritage that, only a century earlier, was shared by flocks of what may have been the most abundant bird of all time.

Four years later the brilliant green-and-yellow Carolina Parakeet, the only parrot native to the United States, became extinct. The last parakeet died in a building next door to Martha's empty house. The Cincinnati Zoo maintains one of these small buildings as a sensitive memorial. It tells the story of all endangered wildlife, while the silent, stuffed pigeons and parakeets mounted there stare back at visitors from cold glass eyes. The establishment of this simple monument in 1977 reflected a nationwide awakening to the threats facing our native wildlife—and a new determination to rescue those species for which there is still time.

Even though we have killed off some of our native species and destroyed the habitats of others, since 1903 we have, as a nation, been setting aside critical lands for threatened wild creatures. That year President Theodore Roosevelt signed an executive order declaring a little island off Florida's east coast to be a refuge for Brown Pelicans and other birds. This act was the beginning of a world-famous system of national wildlife refuges that today includes more than 400 areas in almost every state and territory. State and local governments, as well as private organizations and individuals, have established other refuges for wildlife.

Saving these wild habitats slowed the losses of our native birds, but this action was not enough. In 1973, as a number of species continued to edge toward extinction, our growing concern prompted Congress to pass the Endangered Species Act. Harassing or harming endangered and threatened wildlife became a federal crime.

In addition, the U. S. Fish and Wildlife Service began compiling a list of the wild species that were in serious trouble. The agency also appointed recovery teams of specialists to plan rescue campaigns for many species. By 1983 the number of threatened and endangered birds in the continental United States had grown to 25 species and subspecies, with Hawaii adding 30 more to the list.

In the face of our unending modification of land, water, and wildlife, the wonder is that so many of our native birds still survive. Although the numbers of some are much reduced, more than 650 species regularly nest in North America. The hardy generalists among them adapt to our changes. Cardinals nest in our shrubbery and shade trees, robins go worm hunting on our lawns, and Chimney Swifts turn to our homes instead of hollow trees for nest sites. Our garbage dumps feed the gulls so well that we must seek ways to stem their population explosion.

Crows, among the wariest of all birds, now nest along Constitution Avenue in downtown Washington, D. C., right over the heads of millions of tourists and commuters. In St. Louis a pair of Canada Geese hatched five eggs on the tenth-floor ledge of a bank building. The Giant Canada Goose was believed extinct until scientists discovered a small flock in Minnesota and helped the birds make a comeback. They now thrive in parks within the many cities where they have been transplanted.

The magnificent Wild Turkey was gone from 15 states where it once walked sedately through the deep shade of hardwood forests. But today the turkey is found in every state except Alaska because the forests returned and wildlife biologists found methods of transplanting the birds to their native woodlands and to areas where they had never lived before.

But other birds too specialized to cope with the changing world gradually vanish. These birds merit our deepest concern, in the view of John C. Ogden, an ornithologist and a senior biologist with the National Audubon Society. He works out of a crowded office in Ventura, California. Stacks of reports and maps cover his desk. Charts and pictures decorate the walls. One poster proclaims: CONDORS, HAWKS, OWLS, EAGLES AND TURKEY VULTURES ARE PROTECTED BY FEDERAL AND STATE LAWS. Predominant in the pictures is North America's largest vulture, the California Condor.

Absolute master of the air currents, the 20-pound condor soars effortlessly on wings that span nine feet or more—the longest of any bird on the continent. Wrote one observer: "The strength, the magnificence of their flight . . . the very steadiness of their movement as they soared through constantly changing air currents seemed uncanny."

226

Humans will never look upon their kind again. Swift and graceful Passenger Pigeons (opposite) were once so numerous that Audubon wrote: "The air was literally filled . . . the light of noon-day was obscured as by an eclipse." But hunting and the felling of forests reduced pigeon populations from billions to zero by 1914. The shy Labrador Duck (right), only member of the waterfowl family to disappear in North America, had mysteriously vanished by 1875—before scientists could probe its secret life. The Great Auk (below), a flightless seafarer persecuted for food, oil, and feathers, had become extinct before Audubon died in 1851.

Paintings by John James Audubon, New-York Historical Society

Ogden, whose job is to study the endangered condor, is uncertain about the future of the bird. He sometimes wonders if hope remains for its long-term survival. Or is the ancient glider, after thousands of years on earth, down to its last dozen summers in this overpeopled world?

Long before humans settled here, the ancestors of the condor cast gliding shadows over the last mastodons and saber-toothed cats. After these Pleistocene creatures passed into extinction, the condor soared on to watch the earliest Europeans arrive, bringing the bird a giant step closer to a premature union with the mastodons and sabertooths.

Condors were shot because they were big and easy to hit. They ate poisoned bait that ranchers set out for coyotes and other predators, while egg collectors robbed their nests for museum and hobby collections. Then insecticides caused the birds to lay thin-shelled eggs. And all the time the condors' remaining strongholds shrank. Where they had once drifted over the sky scanning the land for the carcasses of elks and pronghorns, the condors now looked down on citrus groves, alfalfa fields, oil wells, and new towns. And increasingly people disturbed the great birds, even in the mountains where the condors hid their eggs in the shallow, wind-carved recesses of remote sandstone cliffs.

By the late 1970s the facts were obvious: Without dramatic rescue efforts the California Condor, like the Passenger Pigeon, would vanish from the earth. Five agencies, including the U. S. Forest Service, the U. S. Bureau of Land Management, and the California Department of Fish and Game, joined forces to save the condor. The National Audubon Society, long active in efforts to aid the condor, pledged half a million dollars and assigned John Ogden to a last-ditch recovery effort.

The U. S. Fish and Wildlife Service also set aside funds for the project and dispatched Noel Snyder, a research biologist, to serve as Ogden's co-leader at the Condor Research Center. A team of research workers now races time against what many fear is the rapidly approaching extinction of this giant, wild-spirited glider.

"Nobody has a really good grip on how many California Condors there were 200 years ago," Ogden says. "Hundreds for sure." In 1805 Lewis and Clark saw them as far north as northern Oregon, and the birds' range extended south through California.

By the early 1950s only about sixty California Condors lived on the planet. Less than 30 years later, Ogden could say, "We know of five mated pairs and figure only twenty or so condors remain." And they may be disappearing at the rate of two birds a year. If this is so and the losses continue, they could all be gone in the 1990s.

"Even if we identify the problems," Ogden adds, "we may not have time to correct them. We must start a captive breeding program at the same time we are searching for the cause of their troubles. Delaying the captive breeding program might mean we will lose the bird."

There is no hope of a magic recovery. Condors are at least six years old before they begin raising young. They produce only one chick at a time and may spend more than a year raising each youngster. A pair in the wild usually raises only one offspring every other year.

Gathering facts about condors has been painfully slow. On a typical day in the field, Ogden leaves Ventura early, heading toward the dry mountains of the Los Padres or the Angeles National Forests, where fortunate birders sometimes see condors. Throughout the early morning he climbs through the arid country, hiking along a narrow, rocky trail up the chaparral-covered slopes of a rugged canyon.

After miles of climbing, Ogden stops on a mountaintop and looks out over ranks of distant ridges. Across from him, half a mile away, is a small side canyon bristling with the dark green tops of a fir grove. Condors sometimes roost here in the branches of dead trees. Ogden adjusts his straw hat against the blazing sun and settles on the ground beside the trail to wait, hoping to observe the birds and learn more of their secrets. Sometimes the condors come, sometimes they do not. "I never know for certain where they will be," he says.

Condor workers are frustrated by the sheer distances they must travel, the infrequency with which they see condors, and the difficulty of adding bits of new information to their scanty knowledge of these ancient birds. Volunteer condor watchers, serving with the research center, station themselves in little camps half a mile from each known nest. The volunteers maintain constant watch through powerful spotting scopes and record every scrap of condor behavior they can gather.

In 1980 the research team tested a system to speed up its probing of the condor's secrets. To learn more about the movements of California Condors, members flew to Peru and studied the closely related Andean Condor. Working with biologists from the University of Wisconsin, they put small radio transmitters on four South American condors and learned more in one month than they had in 40 years.

Back in California, with the cooperation of the California Department of Fish and Game, the Condor Research Center used large, concealed nets to capture condors. The researchers then fitted the birds with matchbook-size radio transmitters weighing about an ounce and a half. Attached to the leading edge of a wing, the transmitters send beeping signals to radio receiver towers within the condors' range.

"We have the receivers programmed to sweep in all directions on all our frequencies," Ogden says. "We can pick up the signals 80 or 90 miles away. And we can also find the birds from an aircraft."

Information about each bird is transmitted from the towers through telephone lines to Ogden's office in Ventura. "This way we know the map location of each radio-tagged condor throughout the day, enabling us to make computer studies of their daily and seasonal habitats."

These scientists are biologists in a hurry, and their modern research techniques could mean the difference in whether they can prolong the existence of the condor. They made an encouraging discovery in 1982, when a pair of condors began squabbling and knocked their egg off a ledge. The female laid a second egg; this was (*Continued on page 244*)

Victims of human ingenuity, birds confront an array of surprises. Throwaway plastic from a litterbug's six-pack yokes a young Western Gull (opposite). Deadly oil encases a Western Grebe (below) and thousands of other doomed water birds, the victims of accidental spills that damage shorelines and injure delicate ecosystems. Marine birds eat indigestible raw plastic, which resembles the small crustaceans they feed on. Shotgun pellets swallowed by birds inflict fatal lead poisoning on two to three million waterfowl a year. Diving Brown Pelicans snag themselves on fishhooks, eagles are zapped by power lines, and night migrants crash into television towers.

234

Keith H. Murakami, Tom Stack & Associates

235

Pioneering birds from foreign places must muscle their way into their adopted homeland. Darkening the sky like storm clouds, imported European Starlings (left) pirate the nest sites of native birds. Cattle Egrets (below) invaded Florida from South America in the 1940s. Opportunists, they harvested insects, toads, and other prey kicked up by cattle, but quickly learned to follow tractors, which stirred up even more food.

OVERLEAF: An Oriental import prized by hunters, the Ring-necked Pheasant first found a home in the New World in the 1880s. Only ten years later, 50,000 were shot in the first open season. Now Ringnecks live coast to coast.

William J. Weber. Left: Phil and Loretta Hermann, Tom Stack & Associates. Overleaf: Lynn Rogers

Curse or blessing? Alien birds may overwhelm native species, taking food and space for themselves. The majestic Mute Swan (below) was brought to America to grace estates and parks. These hardy aristocrats, long protected for their beauty, spread into the countryside and flourished. Today thousands live wild along the mid-Atlantic coast and around the Great Lakes. At 30 pounds this domineering swan can drown a swimmer or break a person's arm with a blow of its powerful wings.

The less glamorous House Sparrow (opposite), imported from Europe in the 1850s, spread rapidly across the continent. This adaptable bully pushed aside native bluebirds, swallows, wrens, and chickadees, taking possession of their nesting boxes and hollow trees.

A. B. and Robert Arndt. Opposite: Russell C. Hansen

Unable to change their ways, many fragile birds face an uncertain future. In the deep shade of dense western forests, the lumberman's saw threatens the elusive Spotted Owl (opposite). Cutting of mature conifers destroys the homes of wood rats, deer mice, flying squirrels, and insects essential to this hunter of the night. Only a few hundred Kirtland's Warblers (below) still nest beneath young jack pines in their Michigan homeland. The Dusky Seaside Sparrow (right) no longer sings its courtship melody in Florida marshes, its numbers reduced by flooding and by pesticides to a few captive males. (The last female was seen in 1976.) With the passing of the last male, this unobtrusive bird seems destined to join the Passenger Pigeon in oblivion.

spotting scope. But his attention is focused on a pair of brownish gray Sandhill Cranes, each four feet tall and towering on spindly legs above the sedges and bulrushes in the marsh. Drewien studies the cranes through his scope for several minutes. Then a small young bird runs out from beneath one of the tall cranes, crosses an open area, and vanishes into the thick cover. The Whooping Crane chick is dwarfed by the adult Sandhill Cranes, its foster parents. The glimpse is brief, but Drewien plainly sees the splotched, white-and-rust youngster.

This young crane has a special mission. Still in its egg, it had arrived at this lonely Idaho outpost in a heated suitcase, part of a remarkable experiment to build up the world's population of Whooping Cranes.

The drama of the Whooping Crane repeats the tragedy of other birds caught in the path of the advancing human invasion. These majestic white birds, the tallest in North America, evolved in the deep wilderness and could not adjust to the presence of people. Cranes were shot for food and trophies. The wet prairies where they once nested were drained until the birds vanished from their original range, pocket by pocket. After a nonmigratory flock of six Whooping Cranes stopped raising young and disappeared from the marshes of Louisiana, only one small population remained. They nested in the remote marshy wilderness of Wood Buffalo National Park in northern Canada. In 1941 this flock had shrunk to fifteen birds, coming south to winter on the Aransas National Wildlife Refuge along the Texas coast. If it had not been for this refuge, the world's last flock of Whooping Cranes would probably have vanished.

The fate of the Whooping Crane lay heavily on America's conscience. The towering white bird had become a symbol of the threat that we brought to North America's wildlife, a reminder of our poor stewardship and recklessness in dealing with any wild creature that stood in our way.

Massive publicity brought the plight of the cranes to public attention, and fewer were shot along their migration route. Public support for crane conservation programs grew. Today more than a hundred Whooping Cranes keep a precarious toehold on the edge of survival.

In the 1950s scientists began developing a plan to spread Whooping Cranes back over some of the range they once occupied. One idea was to allow Greater Sandhill Cranes, the Whooper's somewhat smaller cousins, to hatch Whooping Crane eggs. The Sandhills, which were plentiful, could serve as foster parents, guiding the young Whoopers through the early months of their lives.

Each nesting pair of wild Whooping Cranes normally produces two eggs. Because of sibling conflicts, however, only one chick usually reaches maturity. The "spare" egg could be slipped from the nests in northern Canada and airlifted in a heated suitcase to Patuxent Wildlife Research Center in Maryland. Here the rare eggs would be turned over to Ray C. Erickson, a research biologist in charge of the center's work with endangered species. His skill led to the building of a population

246

In his secluded quarters at the Los Angeles Zoo, an adult condor waits for a female companion—and the first attempt at indoor mating. Success will help assure the survival of his species. In 1983 the San Diego Zoo hatched the first California Condor in captivity (lower). Its destiny: to produce young for release in the wild.

Though no one would deny that condors may be near the end of their long tenure on earth, opponents of captive breeding argue that humans should work to preserve the birds' vanishing habitat. Will this ungainly chick (below), one of the few hatched in the wild, be one of the last of its kind to grow up and take to the skies? No one knows.

Tupper Ansel Blake, U. S. Fish and Wildlife. Below: Ron Garrison, Zoological Society of San Diego. Right: Kenneth W. Fink, Bruce Coleman Inc.

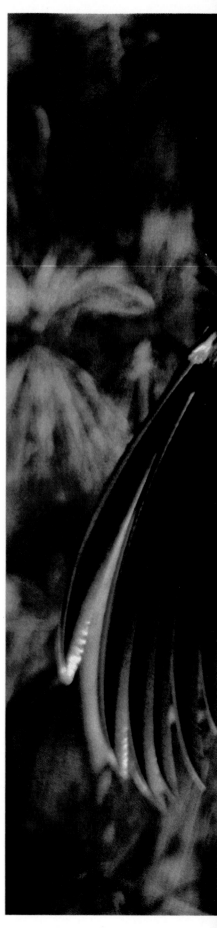

of captive Whooping Cranes at Patuxent. These birds, their eggs, and the eggs taken from wild crane nests would test the foster parent idea.

After years of study, the experiment began in 1975, when 14 eggs were flown from northern Canada to southeastern Idaho. In succeeding years the egg supply increased until 27 Whooping Crane eggs—14 from Canada and 13 from Patuxent—were flown to Grays Lake in the spring of 1982. There Drewien slipped each egg into the nest of a carefully selected pair of Sandhill Cranes. Then, if the egg did not fall victim to coyotes, ravens, or snowstorms, it would probably hatch.

The young Whooping Cranes grow rapidly during their summer at Grays Lake. With their foster parents they fly south as a family to New Mexico, where they winter on and near the Bosque del Apache National Wildlife Refuge. After seven years of work by biologists in the United States and Canada, this newly created Whooping Crane flock has 17 Whoopers mingling with their Sandhill cousins.

The young cranes, lacking the strength and experience of older birds, are more vulnerable to coyotes, shooting, and accidents. Drewien recalls the tragedy of Miracles, the last Whooper hatched at Grays Lake that first year. Miracles had not been seen for a couple of days, so Drewien went looking for him. "I found him entangled in a barbed-wire fence," he says. "I guess he got lazy, and instead of flying over the fence, he jumped into the top wire, got his foot caught, and died of trauma."

Once the Grays Lake population of cranes is established, the Whooping Crane recovery plan calls for creating a third group, perhaps somewhere in the east or midwest. If the biologists can double the number of breeding pairs in the Aransas-Wood Buffalo flock to about 40, while building the new populations to 20 breeding pairs each, the bird will have gained a new degree of security. And the crane workers will feel that they have perhaps won the long struggle to save this rare bird.

Elsewhere, biologists seek ways to save other endangered birds, among them the world's most admired falcon, the Peregrine. High against the summer sky this torpedo-shaped hunter beats the air with its long pointed wings, tilts earthward, and slips into the most spectacular dive any bird can make. Hissing wind slides over the Peregrine's feathers as it gains speed in pursuit of a flying pigeon. Wings half-folded, the falcon slides down the sky at 100 miles an hour, then 150 miles an hour, and still gaining speed! Guided by acute vision, the falcon intercepts its prey and strikes it in midair with its talons. In this spectacular way the Peregrine calls on an ancient genetic inheritance that equips it to take food from the sky.

Filled with energy and gifted with astounding speed, the acrobatic Peregrine, too large, fast, and elusive to be taken by most predators, might seem secure from harm. And in a natural world this is largely so. But after World War II the mighty Peregrine, master of the air, met an enemy that threatened to destroy it. *(Continued on page 258)*

A towering Sandhill Crane (right) acts as foster parent to a fluffy relative, the endangered Whooping Crane. Scientists have found that the more abundant Sandhills can be tricked into hatching and raising their young cousins, like this one in a remote Idaho marsh. When the gawky chick is two months old (below), a biologist carefully fits one of its long legs with an identifying band, which will provide vital data about crane movements.

Ralph Stoor. Right: Roderick C. Drewien

Steven C. Wilson and Karen C. Hayden, Entheos

Though its numbers have increased more than fivefold from a low of 22 in 1941, the Whooping Crane still needs a helping hand. Wild and wary, the once-doomed bird finds safety on its Texas wintering grounds, a national wildlife refuge on the Gulf of Mexico.

The bird that got a second chance: Nearly extinct by 1900, the Wild Turkey now roams forests near major eastern cities. America's largest game bird flourished in colonial days; Benjamin Franklin proposed it as our national symbol in 1776. Then the elusive turkey all but vanished as settlers cleared its forest haunts and slaughtered it for food. Modern biologists discovered that wild birds, hardy and adaptable, could be trapped and transplanted to their ancestral range and beyond—to every state but Alaska.

For the gobbler (below), capable of flying 55 miles an hour, the price of survival is constant alertness. With a running stride of four feet, a turkey can outdistance a dog or a fox—and can even swim. Young turkeys (opposite) face the greatest risks. Before they can fly, the poults must roost on the ground. When a few weeks old and capable of flight, they follow their mother to a nighttime refuge in the trees. Her broad wings shelter the youngsters from predators and the weather.

This threat came with the insecticides that we began spreading on our farmlands. Predatory birds near the top of their food chains ingested pesticides with their prey and soon built up threatening levels of poison residues in their bodies. Peregrine Falcons were among the early victims, and the stricken birds were no longer rearing chicks on the remote cliffside ledges where they had lived for countless centuries. Peregrines disappeared everywhere east of the Mississippi River, and their numbers plummeted in the west as well.

Where the falcons still attempted to produce young, their eggs failed to hatch or broke in the nest beneath the parent's weight. This failure led to the discovery by a British scientist that the eggs had abnormally thin shells. The cause was traced to pesticides, especially DDE, a breakdown product of DDT. The presence of these chemicals altered the supply of female sex hormones that control the calcium available for making eggshells. DDT was also blamed for reducing to dangerously low levels the numbers of Brown Pelicans, Ospreys, Bald Eagles, and other birds. Evidence against DDT became so overwhelming that, in 1972, the federal government banned its general use. The environment began a long, slow cleansing process.

At Cornell University in Ithaca, New York, Tom J. Cade, a noted ornithologist and an admirer of falcons, decided that it was possible to restore the Peregrines to the American skies. Cade supervised the construction of a falcon-breeding barn at Cornell, and falconers lent him three pairs of Peregrine Falcons.

In 1973, its third year of operation, the barn hatched 20 Peregrine chicks in incubators. Hundreds of supporters began contributing to Cade's project, which was organized as the Peregrine Fund. The idea worked so well that the fund now has two other breeding facilities—one in Santa Cruz, California, the other at Fort Collins, Colorado. By 1983 these three Peregrine facilities were producing more than 250 young falcons a year for release in the wild.

According to William A. Burnham, who manages the Rocky Mountain program for the Peregrine Fund, there were only ten known Peregrine nests in all of Colorado when the conservation group started work there in 1974. A year later Burnham began collecting eggs from a single pair of borrowed Peregrines. The eggs went into a small incubator that he kept in his bedroom. Every second hour throughout the day and night, Burnham turned the eggs, as the natural parents would do.

From the few wild nests in the Rocky Mountains, Burnham and his team also collected the thin-shelled eggs that would have broken under the parents, then replaced each egg with one made of wood putty. The real eggs went into the incubators for hatching, and the young falcons were later traded back to their parents in exchange for the bogus eggs.

Gradually the numbers of captive Peregrines increased. During the egg-laying period, Burnham or a member of his staff kept close watch over a bank of television screens that monitored every loft and its pair of adult falcons. Each new egg was quickly collected for the incubators.

A critical test came on that special day when the incubator-hatched falcons were set free. The Peregrine teams used an ancient falconry technique known as hacking. The birds, still too young to fly, were installed in a box on a cliffside. Food was dropped to them through a tube so they did not associate humans with eating. Eventually, the front of the box was left open, and the young falcons were free to fly.

The young Peregrines have been released from towers on coastal marshes and even from tall buildings in cities, where the falcons feed on pigeons. Birds set free in this program now raise wild young of their own, and the lordly falcon is returning to its historic nesting sites. "I think people want to assist with this program because they are inspired by a bird that lives and raises its young on the sheer faces of high cliffs and dives at speeds of almost 200 miles an hour," says Burnham.

Lessons learned from the Peregrine work can be applied to other endangered species, including our national bird, the powerful Bald Eagle. The fierce-looking bird with the gleaming white head and tail once flourished across the United States and Canada. Today, although still abundant in Alaska, the Bald Eagle is in trouble in 48 states—another victim of the thin-shell syndrome.

Before DDT was used, New York had more than 70 breeding pairs of Bald Eagles; by 1965 the state was down to its last pair. With the blessing of the U. S. Fish and Wildlife Service, biologists from the New York Department of Environmental Conservation set up a hacking program in 1976 and began releasing young eagles shipped in from the Great Lakes region, Maryland, and Alaska. The scientists installed the birds in cages perched on towers and permitted them, when old enough, to fly free. This plan worked, as it had for the Peregrines. In 1980 two of the eagles mated, built their first nest, and raised two chicks—the first known eaglets hatched by wild parents in New York in nearly ten years.

After rebuilding the state's eagle population to 40 breeding pairs, New York expects to turn its efforts to other endangered wildlife. Eagle transplants are under way in other states, and the Bald Eagle shows signs of recovery in many of these areas.

Another success story has unfolded in the Centennial Valley of southwestern Montana. Miles of winding, unpaved road lead into this secluded valley, etched by the meandering path of the Red Rock River and its tributary creeks. Across the broad marshes and meadows wander huge black moose, fleet-footed pronghorns, graceful shorebirds, and high-stepping Sandhill Cranes.

Pairs of Trumpeter Swans, necks outstretched, fly low across the marsh. Their distant calls, drifting back over the valley, are haunting reminders of the voices once heard along many wilderness waterways. When flatboats carried pioneers down the Ohio River, the settlers probably saw Trumpeter Swans, plentiful in those faraway days. Perhaps, too, the settlers shot the low-flying giants for food.

Shooting a Trumpeter Swan must have filled the family provider on the frontier with elation. One easy shot brought down the biggest of the world's seven swan species, the largest waterfowl anywhere, the heaviest bird native to North America. The male swan weighed 30 pounds or so and had a wingspread of eight feet. From the tip of its black bill to the end of its white tail, this regal bird measured six feet in length.

Wherever the swans were found, they were taken for feathers and food. A market even developed for their soft skins, which were fashioned into powder puffs. Then, as people pushed deeper and deeper into the continent, they drained the marshes where the swans often built their bulky nests on the tops of muskrat houses.

This deadly combination of guns and drainage erased the swans from their native range until, by 1900, few people saw or heard them any longer. In 1912 a noted ornithologist, Edward H. Forbush, wrote of the Trumpeter Swan: "Its total extinction is now only a matter of years."

The last Trumpeters south of the Canadian border lived on, however, hidden in the wild and remote Centennial Valley, across the mountains along Henrys Fork of the Snake River, and in nearby Yellowstone National Park. Forbush's doleful prediction might have come true except that in 1935, when fewer than a hundred Trumpeter Swans remained in the mid-continent population, the heart of the Centennial Valley became the Red Rock Lakes National Wildlife Refuge. The refuge included hot springs that kept two ponds free of ice throughout the bitter winters, providing the birds with a feeding area.

Given protection and some supplemental winter feeding, the swans began to rebuild their numbers in the Centennial Valley. For the past two decades this population has held fairly stable.

Surplus Trumpeters have been moved to other refuges in the United States, and plans call for spreading the birds still more widely across their original range. The mid-continent population has grown to a thousand or more, while others have held on in the wilderness regions of Canada and Alaska. Trumpeter Swan is one of the few names we have been able to remove from the list of rare birds.

Perhaps other species will be equally fortunate, but the cost of rescuing wild creatures from the edge of extinction is heavy. As the numbers of rare and endangered species grow, economic realities limit the resources we can apply to the task.

Our attitudes toward wildlife have changed in recent times. It is no longer legal to kill birds for hat feathers, to collect their eggs as a hobby, or to hang "chicken hawks" from farm fences. Instead, a growing number of people now take binoculars in hand and go bird watching for the fun of it. The ranks of these bird watchers grow yearly, and so does the membership of bird clubs and environmental groups.

Yet the big threat remains. Human populations destroy the birds' habitats. But if our increasing concern leads to preserving their habitats, we may indeed extend the time that birds in wide variety and good numbers will enrich the world with their flashing colors and wild songs.

In her aerie atop a Baltimore skyscraper (left), Scarlett confronts a smaller male brought in as her potential mate. Until she chooses a partner, biologists will gently replace Scarlett's infertile eggs each spring with young falcons hatched in captivity. Scarlett feeds and raises her foster family in her high-rise home (below). By summer's end the youngsters will have exchanged their downy covering for new feathers and launched themselves on their first flight.

Michael Ventura (also left)

To help the Peregrine Falcon's comeback, scientists incubate a healthy, brown egg as well as one that is thin shelled because of chemical poisoning (upper). Until recently, chicks were fed through a parent look-alike—a hand puppet (left). The purpose: to prevent the chicks from relying on people for food when the birds are set free.

But researchers learned that these young birds will not form a dependency on people during the first two weeks of life, so humans no longer have to masquerade as Peregrines. When the five-week-old falcons near flight age, they are moved to boxes, from which they will soar free ten days later to join their wild brethren.

OVERLEAF: *Trumpeter Swans, remnants of the huge flocks that blanketed the skies 200 years ago, take to the air in western Washington.*

Frans Lanting (all). Overleaf: Art Wolfe

Hunters and settlers of the 19th century made "a vanishing race" of the Trumpeter Swan; scientists of the 20th century have helped rescue the regal bird. With the sun as a light source, a field biologist (left) takes an inside look at the condition of a swan's egg. Grain from bulk feeders (upper) helps the birds survive bitter Montana winters. Colored neckbands and numbers (lower) help conservationists recognize individual swans from afar.

OVERLEAF: *America's first symbol of an imperiled species, the Trumpeter Swan has become a hopeful sign of man's concern for the other creatures sharing this planet.*

Jeff Foott (all). Overleaf: Wayne Lankinen

About the Authors

Frank Graham, Jr., is a field editor of *Audubon* who lives in Milbridge, Maine. Graham has written many books and articles on conservation and ecology. His most recent book is *Gulls: An Ecological History.*

Louis J. Halle pursues his lifelong interests in natural history and writing in Geneva, Switzerland, where he retired after a career with the U. S. State Department and as a professor of politics. His book *Birds against Men* won the John Burroughs Medal for distinguished nature writing. Other books include *Spring in Washington* and *Out of Chaos.*

Paul A. Johnsgard is the Foundation Professor of Life Sciences at the University of Nebraska in Lincoln. He has written many books and articles on birds, often illustrating them with his own drawings. His latest book is *Hummingbirds of North America.*

Anne LaBastille, a wildlife ecologist and writer, has contributed stories to NATIONAL GEOGRAPHIC, *Audubon, Natural History,* and other publications. Her book *Woodswoman* chronicles her life in the Adirondacks of New York, where she lives in a log cabin she built herself.

George Laycock is a field editor of *Audubon.* He has written more than 35 books, including *Autumn of the Eagle, The Bird Watcher's Bible,* and most recently, *The Ohio Valley,* which he wrote with his wife. He lives in Cincinnati, Ohio.

Roger F. Pasquier has been watching birds since he was seven. He works in the Division of Birds at the Smithsonian Institution in Washington, D. C., where he is executive assistant to the president of the International Council for Bird Preservation. His articles have appeared in *Natural History, Nature Conservancy News, Smithsonian,* and other magazines. He is the author of *Watching Birds.*

Franklin Russell has traveled the world to write about wildlife. His books include *Watchers at the Pond, The Secret Islands,* and his newest work, *The Hunting Animal.* A native New Zealander, Russell now lives in Manhattan, where he studies baroque music in his spare time.

Acknowledgments & Bibliography

We would like to thank the individuals who generously contributed their time and knowledge. Our special thanks go to Eirik A. T. Blom; Jon L. Dunn; Lise M. Swinson, National Geographic Society; and George E. Watson, Smithsonian Institution.

We are also indebted to George W. Archibald, International Crane Foundation; Jody Bolt, National Geographic Society; Richard G. B. Brown and Anthony R. Lock, Canadian Wildlife Service; William A. Burnham, The Peregrine Fund, Inc.; John Byelich; Eugene A. Cardiff, San Bernardino County Museum; John V. Dennis; Roderick C. Drewien, University of Idaho; Ray C. Erickson; Alan Feduccia, University of North Carolina; John W. Fitzpatrick, Field Museum of Natural History; Steven L. Hilty; Francis M. Hueber, Smithsonian Institution; Frank Y. Larkin; M. Ross Lein, University of Calgary; Judith W. McIntyre, Syracuse University; Frank McKinney, University of Minnesota; Rees L. Madsen, Red Rock Lakes National Wildlife Refuge; and Peter R. Marler, Rockefeller University Field Center.

Also Harold Mayfield; Harvey W. Miller, U. S. Fish and Wildlife Service; Eugene S. Morton, National Zoological Park; J. Peter Myers and Robert S. Ridgely, Academy of Natural Sciences; Peter E. Nye, New York State Department of Environmental Conservation; John C. Ogden, National Audubon Society; Ray B. Owen, University of Maine; Dennis R. Paulson, University of Washington; Robert Randall; John H. Rappole, Texas A and I University; John G. Sidle, Arrowwood National Wildlife Refuge; Robert W. Storer, University of Michigan; Robert B. Waide, University of Puerto Rico; Jeffrey R. Walters, North Carolina State University; and Lawrence Zeleny.

We are also indebted to the staffs of the places listed in the guide to "Bird Watching by State and Province" and to the Canadian Wildlife Service, Manomet Bird Observatory, National Geographic Society Library, USF&G Insurance, U. S. Fish and Wildlife Service, and World Wildlife Fund.

Books of a general nature included *Birds and Their Attributes* by Glover Morrill Allen, *Life Histories of North American Birds* by Arthur Cleveland Bent, *Waterfowl of North America* by Paul A. Johnsgard, *The Birdwatcher's Companion* by Christopher Leahy, *Handbook of North American Birds* edited by Ralph S. Palmer, *Watching Birds* by Roger F. Pasquier, *The Audubon Society Encyclopedia of North American Birds* by John K. Terres, *A New Dictionary of Birds* edited by A. Landsborough Thomson, and *The Life of Birds* by Joel Carl Welty.

We also consulted *The Birds of Canada* by W. Earl Godfrey, *The Bird Life of Texas* by Harry C. Oberholser, *A Field Guide to the Birds of Eastern and Central North America* and *A Field Guide to Western Birds* by Roger Tory Peterson, and *Birds of North America* by Chandler S. Robbins, Bertel Bruun, and Herbert S. Zim.

Helpful references about evolution included *The Age of Birds* by Alan Feduccia.

Books about birds in spring were *A Field Guide to the Nests, Eggs, and Nestlings of North American Birds* by Colin Harrison and *Those of the Gray Wind: The Sandhill Cranes* by Paul A. Johnsgard.

For information on birdlife in summer we relied on *The Family Life of Birds* by Hans D. Dossenbach and *Parent Birds and Their Young* by Alexander F. Skutch.

Accounts of fall migration included *The Migrations of Birds* by Jean Dorst, *Bird Migration* by Donald R. Griffin, and *Migration of Birds* by Frederick C. Lincoln.

For material on winter birds we used *Migrant Birds in the Neotropics* edited by Allen Keast and Eugene S. Morton.

Conservation readings included *Man's Dominion* by Frank Graham, Jr., *The Alien Animals* by George Laycock, *Man and the California Condor* by Ian McMillan, *The Whooping Crane* by Faith McNulty, *The Kirtland's Warbler* by Harold Mayfield, and *To Save a Bird in Peril* by David R. Zimmerman.

We also used the following periodicals: *American Birds, Audubon, The Condor, Journal of Field Ornithology, The Living Bird Quarterly,* NATIONAL GEOGRAPHIC, *National Wildlife, Natural History, Scientific American,* and *Smithsonian.*

The sites described in this guide represent a selection of special bird-watching spots that you can easily visit. We have included a variety of habitats and birdlife, but we have only touched the highlights. For more information write to the address listed with the entry. To find the best bird-watching places in a specific area, contact the local National Audubon Society chapter, bird club, or natural history museum.

These abbreviations and terms appear in our guide:
Alcids - includes auks, murres, puffins, and guillemots.
Land birds - raptors, songbirds, and other species that do not habitually frequent aquatic or marine habitats.
Marsh birds - gallinules, rails, coots, bitterns, and other birds that feed and nest in marshes.
Raptors - hawks and owls.
Seabirds - shearwaters, petrels, albatrosses, and other birds that frequent the open ocean.
Shorebirds - includes plovers, phalaropes, and sandpipers.
Songbirds - perching birds, such as warblers and sparrows.
Wading birds - long-legged water birds that wade for food, such as herons and cranes.
Water birds - includes pelicans, loons, grebes, gulls, and terns.
Waterfowl - ducks, geese, and swans.

NF - National Forest
NM - National Monument
NP - National Park
NS - National Seashore
NWR - National Wildlife Refuge
PP - Provincial Park
SP - State Park

United States

Alabama
Dauphin Island Sanctuary, Box 608, Dauphin Island 36528. Staging area in spring (late February-May) and fall (September-November) for land birds migrating across the Gulf of Mexico. Winter haven for shorebirds and ducks.

Wheeler NWR, Box 1643, Decatur 35602. Ducks, geese, and water birds abundant from mid-October to early February. Spring warbler migration peaks in mid-April.

Alaska
Denali NP and Preserve, Box 9, Denali National Park 99755. Spring and summer breeding ground for shorebirds and land birds, including Lesser Golden-Plovers and Water Pipits.

Glacier Bay NP and Preserve, Gustavus 99826. May and June bring migrating water birds, shorebirds, and land birds. A wide array of alcids and water birds, such as Tufted Puffins and Black-legged Kittiwakes, nest here from May to August.

Kenai NWR, Box 2139, Soldotna 99669. Nesting area for Bald Eagles, Arctic Terns, Red-necked Phalaropes, and a dozen kinds of waterfowl.

Arizona
Arizona-Sonora Desert Museum, Rt. 9, Tucson 85743. Plants and wildlife in natural settings, including a walk-through aviary where roadrunners and other desert species live.

Cave Creek Canyon, near Portal. For information: Arizona-Sonora Desert Museum, Rt. 9, Tucson 85743. Many western species, such as Band-tailed Pigeons and Hutton's Vireos. Breeding area for rare Elegant Trogons.

Chiricahua NM, Dos Cabezas Rt., Willcox 85643. Plain and Bridled Titmice, Strickland's Woodpeckers, and some Mexican birds common all year.

Organ Pipe Cactus NM, Rt. 1, Ajo 85321. Desert birds of the southwest, including Gila Woodpeckers, Phainopeplas, Pyrrhuloxias, and roadrunners.

Patagonia-Sonoita Creek Sanctuary, Box 815, Patagonia 85624. Breeding ground for Mexican species, including Zone-tailed and Gray Hawks. Many hawks, Golden Eagles, and sparrows winter here.

Ramsey Canyon Preserve, Rt. 1, Hereford 85615. Spring and summer mecca for some 15 species of hummingbirds.

Arkansas
White River NWR, Box 308, DeWitt 72042. Large flocks of waterfowl from mid-November to late February. Migrating shorebirds and songbirds, mainly warblers, in April and May. Contact refuge manager for permission to visit.

California
Joshua Tree NM, 74485 National Monument Drive, Twentynine Palms 92277. Phainopeplas nest in spring and summer, Gambel's Quail and roadrunners in April and early May. Transient warblers pass through in spring and fall.

Klamath Basin NWRs (Bear Valley, Clear Lake, Klamath Forest, Lower Klamath, Tule Lake, Upper Klamath), Rt. 1, Tulelake 96134. Stunning concentrations of migrating Snow Geese, Ross' Geese, and other waterfowl, including arctic-nesting species, in October, November, and early March. Water birds and raptors nest here from May to July. Largest number of wintering Bald Eagles outside Alaska.

Merced NWR, Box 2176, Los Banos 93635. Wintering area for freshwater ducks, Ross' Geese, Sandhill Cranes, and other water-loving species.

Monterey Bay. Favored by shearwaters and petrels from August to October; loons, grebes, and ducks in spring, fall, winter; shorebirds, alcids, gulls, and terns year round.

Mount Pinos Condor Observation Site, near Gorman. For information: Condor Research Center, 87 North Chestnut Street, Ventura 93001. Rare California Condors visible year round, especially between July and September.

Point Reyes NS, Point Reyes 94956. Famed for land bird migrants in fall. Waterfowl winter from November to February. Common Murres, Pelagic Cormorants, and Pigeon Guillemots nest on cliffsides.

Sacramento NWR, Rt. 1, Willows 95988. From October through January hundreds of thousands of ducks and Snow Geese. Vast flocks of shorebirds from August to October.

Salton Sea NWR, Box 120, Calipatria 92233. Tens of thousands of waterfowl and shorebirds from January to March. Red-winged and Yellow-headed Blackbirds, as well as other migrant songbirds, stop in March and April. In summer the west's largest population of nesting doves.

Yosemite NP, Box 577, Yosemite National Park 95389. Birdlife spans all the habitats of the Sierra Nevada, ranging from rapids inhabited by American Dippers to forests alive with Great Gray Owls and Steller's Jays to snowfields favored by Rosy Finches.

Colorado
Alamosa/Monte Vista NWR, Box 1148, Alamosa 81101. A major nesting area for waterfowl. Main stopover in spring and fall for young Whooping Cranes migrating between New Mexico and Idaho with their foster parents—Sandhill Cranes.

Pawnee National Grasslands, near Greeley. For information: U. S. Forest Service, 2009 Ninth Street, Greeley 80631. Lapland Longspurs, Lark Buntings, Horned Larks, and other prairie species nest from May to July. Excellent views of Golden Eagles and other raptors in fall and early winter.

Rocky Mountain NP, Estes Park 80517. Late May through July is the best time to see an astonishing variety of mountain and tundra species, including Water Pipits, Rosy Finches, and White-tailed Ptarmigan.

Connecticut

Hammonasset Beach SP, Box 271, Madison 06443. Migrating land birds in May; shorebirds in May, August, and September; raptors, especially falcons, in fall; water birds and waterfowl in late fall and winter.

Salt Meadow NWR, Old Clinton Road, Westbrook. For information: Ninigret NWR, Box 307, Charlestown, RI 02813. Migrating warblers and other songbirds in spring, hawks in late September and early October.

Delaware

Bombay Hook NWR, Rt. 1, Smyrna 19977. Look for hawks year round, immense flocks of geese and other waterfowl from February to April and from September to December, and many species of shorebirds in May and from July to October.

Florida

Corkscrew Swamp Sanctuary, Rt. 6, Naples 33999. Herons, egrets, ibis, and other swamp dwellers abundant from December to May. One of North America's largest colonies of Wood Storks.

Everglades NP, Box 279, Homestead 33030. Most North American species of water-loving birds, including pelicans, egrets, and Anhingas, common year round. Winter refuge for songbirds and raptors.

J. N. "Ding" Darling NWR, One Wildlife Drive, Sanibel 33957. Wading birds abundant all year long. Thousands of shorebirds and songbirds pass through in spring and fall, mainly in April and November.

Loxahatchee NWR, Rt. 1, Boynton Beach 33437. Endangered Snail Kites can sometimes be seen from November to April. Wintering area for waterfowl, raptors, and songbirds.

St. Marks NWR, Box 68, St. Marks 32355. Florida's major wintering area for waterfowl. Bald Eagles nest in December and January. Migrating shorebirds common in late spring and early fall.

Georgia

Okefenokee NWR, Rt. 2, Folkston 31537. Spring breeding area for Wood Ducks, Barred Owls, woodpeckers, songbirds, and Sandhill Cranes and other wading birds. Winter refuge for ducks.

Savannah NWR, Box 8487, Savannah 31412. Look for Anhingas, White Ibis, herons, and egrets year round. Summer breeding ground for Purple Gallinules. About 15 species of wintering ducks.

Idaho

Bear Lake NWR, 370 Webster Street, Montpelier 83254. Canada Geese, Canvasbacks, Redheads, and shorebirds breed here in spring and summer.

Grays Lake NWR, Wayan 83285. From early April to mid-October the breeding ground of an experimental flock of Sandhill Cranes with their foster chicks—endangered Whooping Cranes.

Illinois

Chautauqua NWR, Rt. 2, Havana 62644. Look for large numbers of Mallards and other ducks from mid-March to April and from mid-November to December. Shorebirds in late August and early September.

Chicago lakefront. Numerous parks in view of Chicago's skyline shelter ducks and geese in winter and attract migrant land birds, shorebirds, water birds, and waterfowl in spring and fall.

Indiana

Muscatatuck NWR, Box 631, Seymour 47274. Magnet for migrating waterfowl and water birds in March and November. Nesting area for Wood Ducks and songbirds.

Iowa

De Soto NWR, Rt. 1, Missouri Valley 51555. Multitudes of Snow Geese and ducks, mainly Mallards, in October and November. Bald Eagles winter here from November to March.

Union Slough NWR, Rt. 1, Titonka 50480. Concentrations of shorebirds in late summer and early fall, waterfowl in April and October.

Kansas

Cheyenne Bottoms Wildlife Area, Rt. 3, Great Bend 67530. One of the largest gatherings of waterfowl on the Central flyway, mainly in February, March, and October. Migrant shorebirds touch down in April, May, and from late July to September.

Kirwin NWR, Kirwin 67644. Migrating Sandhill Cranes, shorebirds, and waterfowl in spring (February to mid-March) and fall (September to mid-October). Winter haven for waterfowl. Eastern and western varieties of grebes, phoebes, and other species nest here from mid-April to September.

Quivira NWR, Box G, Stafford 67578. Thousands of Sandhill Cranes, Canada Geese, white-fronted geese, Mallards, and other migrants from late November to December and from February to early April.

Kentucky

Mammoth Cave NP, Mammoth Cave 42259. Noted for songbirds, especially wood warblers; best to visit in late spring or early summer.

Reelfoot NWR - See Tennessee.

Louisiana

Sabine NWR, M.R.H. Box 107, Hackberry 70645. Mecca for Snow Geese, shorebirds, and ducks in winter, especially December and January. Large nesting colonies of wading birds. Migrant birds flock along nearby coast of *Cameron Parish* in spring and fall.

Maine

Acadia NP, Box 177, Bar Harbor 04609. Summertime breeding locale for warblers and other songbirds. Large rafts of Common Eiders in winter.

Baxter SP, 64 Balsam Drive, Millinocket 04462. Spruce Grouse, Gray Jays, and other northern species nest here.

Monhegan Island, near Boothbay Harbor. For information: Maine Audubon Society, 118 Rt. 1, Falmouth 04105. Late September is best time to see land bird migrants and species that have wandered or been blown off course. Island can be reached by ferry.

Maryland

Blackwater NWR, Rt. 1, Cambridge 21613. Waterfowl mass here from mid-October through November and from mid-February through March; thousands stay for the winter. Bald Eagles year round.

Eastern Neck NWR, Rt. 2, Rock Hall 21661. A major feeding and resting place for migrant waterfowl, including American Black Ducks, in fall, winter, and spring. Thousands of Canada Geese winter at nearby *Remington Farms.*

Massachusetts

Great Meadows NWR, Weir Hill Road, Sudbury 01776. Inland oasis for wildlife within a few miles of Boston. Attracts transient warblers in May, migrant waterfowl in spring and fall, and nesting water birds and songbirds in summer.

Parker River NWR, Northern Boulevard, Plum Island, Newburyport 01950. Migrant shorebirds in July and August, waterfowl in October and November, and seabirds from September through April.

Michigan

Seney NWR, Seney 49883. Canada Geese and their young can be seen from June through September. Sandhill Cranes stop in September and October.

Whitefish Point Bird Observatory. For information: Michigan Audubon Society, 7000 North Westnedge, Kalamazoo 49007. In early May look for thousands of migrating loons, waterfowl, and raptors.

Minnesota

Agassiz NWR, Middle River 56737. Large numbers of nesting Canada Geese, gulls, cormorants, and other water-loving species. Waterfowl in spring, summer, and fall.

Hawk Ridge Nature Reserve, Skyline Parkway, Duluth. For information: Duluth Audubon Society, Biology Department, University of Minnesota, Duluth 55812. Excellent view of migrating hawks from September to November; peak flight of Broadwings during third week of September.

Rice Lake NWR, Rt. 2, McGregor 55760. Water birds nest on islands. Ring-necked Ducks and other waterfowl stop here in fall and early winter.

Mississippi

Noxubee NWR, Rt. 1, Brooksville 39739. Look for large numbers of woodpeckers, including the endangered Red-cockaded, and other woodland birds year round, waterfowl and Bald Eagles in winter.

Yazoo NWR, Rt. 1, Hollandale 38748. Wood Ducks abundant year round, waterfowl in winter.

Missouri

Mingo NWR, Rt. 1, Puxico 63960. March, October, and November bring large numbers of waterfowl, mainly Mallards and other ducks. Many ducks and Canada Geese winter here from October to January.

Squaw Creek NWR, Box 101, Mound City 64470. Stopover for white pelicans in April and October and for hundreds of thousands of waterfowl, mainly Snow Geese and Mallards, in November and early December. Bald Eagles come in December to feed on fish and waterfowl.

Montana

Bowdoin NWR, Box J, Malta 59538. Canada Geese, Great Blue Herons, cormorants, gulls, and white pelicans breed from mid-April to late September.

Glacier NP, West Glacier 59936. Noted for ptarmigan and four other resident species of grouse: Sharp-tailed, Ruffed, Blue, and Spruce. Bald Eagles feed on spawning salmon in October and November.

Medicine Lake NWR, Medicine Lake 59247. Water birds, waterfowl, shorebirds, and upland prairie species are nesting here by early June. Migrating Tundra Swans, Sandhill Cranes, Franklin's Gulls, and hundreds of thousands of waterfowl stop in spring and fall.

Red Rock Lakes NWR, Monida Star Rt., Lima 59739. Year-round refuge for Trumpeter Swans. Nesting area for Sandhill Cranes, Long-billed Curlews, Willets, and many species of ducks. Large numbers of migrant waterfowl, including Tundra Swans, arrive after October 15.

Nebraska

Platte River Valley. Enormous gatherings of Sandhill Cranes in spring, waterfowl in spring and fall. Wintering Bald Eagles from November to March.

Nevada

Ruby Lake NWR, Ruby Valley 89833. Trumpeter Swans, wading birds, and more than a dozen varieties of ducks, mainly Canvasbacks and Redheads, nest here from late April to July.

Stillwater NWR, Box 1236, Fallon 89406. Vast numbers of migrating ducks in spring (March-April) and fall (October-November), transient shorebirds in August and September. Ducks, Canada Geese, shorebirds, and other water-loving species breed here from late April through July.

New Hampshire

Wapack NWR, Peterborough. For information: Administrator, Great Meadows NWR, Weir Hill Road, Sudbury, MA 01776. Ideal nesting habitat for migrant songbirds, especially White-throated Sparrows, Winter Wrens, Swainson's Thrushes, and warblers.

New Jersey

Brigantine NWR, Great Creek Road, Oceanville 08231. Concentrations of water-loving birds in all seasons, especially waterfowl in fall, shorebirds and wading birds in spring and fall.

Cape May Point. For information: Cape May Bird Observatory, Box 3, Cape May Point 08212. Strong northwest winds and a sudden drop in temperature bring large, southward-bound flocks of land birds, water birds, waterfowl, and shorebirds from late July until December. Raptor flights peak in early October.

New Mexico

Bitter Lake NWR, Box 7, Roswell 88201. Winter haven for water birds and waterfowl, including Sandhill Cranes, Snow Geese, and ducks. Roadrunners and other birds of the southwest common all year.

Bosque del Apache NWR, Rt. 1, Socorro 87801. Wintering area from October through February for ducks, Snow Geese, and a flock of endangered Whooping Cranes with their foster parents—Sandhill Cranes.

New York

Derby Hill, Sage Creek Drive, Pulaski. Excellent lookout for migrating hawks in spring and waterfowl in fall.

Jamaica Bay Wildlife Refuge, Gateway National Recreation Area, Floyd Bennett Field, Brooklyn 11234. From early April to October, concentrations of water-loving species and land birds within sight of Manhattan skyscrapers. Migrant ducks and shorebirds in spring and fall.

Sapsucker Woods Sanctuary, 159 Sapsucker Woods Road, Ithaca 14850. Large numbers and many varieties of migrant ducks and water birds stop in spring and fall. Songbirds nest from mid-May through June.

North Carolina

Cape Hatteras NS, Box 675, Manteo 27954. Renowned wintering area for Snow Geese, Canada Geese, and Brant. Impressive numbers of seabirds in spring and fall, shorebirds in mid-May and August.

North Dakota

Souris Loop NWRs (Des Lacs, J. Clark Salyer, Lostwood, Upper Souris). For information: Refuge Manager, J. Clark Salyer NWR, Upham 58789. Grebes, herons, and other water birds nest in May and June. Migrating Sandhill Cranes and Snow Geese stop in mid-April, ducks in mid-April and early October, warblers in late April and May, and shorebirds from late April through May and from late July through August.

Ohio

Ottawa NWR, 14000 West State, Rt. 2, Oak Harbor 43449. Vast numbers of migrating waterfowl in spring and fall, especially Tundra Swans in early spring. Rookery for thousands of nesting herons.

Oklahoma

Tishomingo NWR, Rt. 1, Tishomingo 73460. Large numbers of water birds and waterfowl gather in late summer and fall. Many waterfowl, as well as eagles and hawks, stay through winter. Scissor-tailed Flycatchers abundant from spring to fall.

Oregon

Malheur NWR, Box 113, Burns 97720. Large numbers and many varieties of migrant songbirds in May, water birds in spring (March-April) and fall (September-October). Sandhill Cranes and Trumpeter Swans nest from May through July.

Pennsylvania

Hawk Mountain Sanctuary, Rt. 2, Kempton 19529. World-famous spot to watch large flights of migrating hawks from late August to early December.

Presque Isle SP, Box 8510, Erie 16505. Migrating land birds in late April and May; shorebirds, waterfowl, and water birds in spring and fall.

Raccoon Creek SP, Hookstown 15050. Look for migrating warblers in May, nesting land birds in summer, and woodpeckers year round.

Rhode Island

Block Island NWR, Box 307, Charlestown 02813. Waterfowl and other migrants stop here in spring (late April-May) and fall (late September-early October). Noted for abundance of land birds in early October.

South Carolina

Cape Romain NWR, Rt. 1, Awendaw 29429. Spectacular concentrations of waterfowl in winter, migrant shorebirds in spring and fall. Prime place to see nesting Black Skimmers and American Oystercatchers.

Savannah NWR — See Georgia.

South Dakota

Sand Lake NWR, Columbia 57433. Spectacular gatherings of migrating waterfowl in April and October. Large numbers of water-loving birds and hawks breed here in June and July.

Waubay NWR, Rt. 1, Waubay 57273. Migrating warblers and sparrows in spring; nesting grebes, including Rednecks, in spring and summer. Attracts eastern and western varieties of bluebirds and other species.

Tennessee

Reelfoot NWR, Rt. 2, Union City 38261. Look for Bald Eagles and spectacular numbers of waterfowl from mid-October to March, huge flocks of blackbirds in late fall and winter, and many species of warblers in spring and fall.

Texas

Anahuac NWR, Box 278, Anahuac 77514. Noted for rails in winter and spring, waterfowl from November to January, and shorebirds and wading birds year round.

Aransas NWR, Box 100, Austwell 77950. From October to May a winter home for wild Whooping Cranes.

Galveston Island. For information: Houston Audubon Society, 440 Wilchester, Houston 77079. Gathering place for countless water birds, waterfowl, and shorebirds. Immense flocks of land birds congregate at nearby *High Island* in April and early May.

Laguna Atascosa NWR, Box 450, Rio Hondo 78583. Winter haven for Redheads and hundreds of thousands of other waterfowl. Spectacular flights of migrating flycatchers, swallows, and other small land birds in March and April. Nesting area for herons and Black-bellied Whistling Ducks.

Rockport. For information: Chamber of Commerce, Box 1055, Rockport 78382. Attracts concentrations of waterfowl from October through April, shorebirds from February through April, hawks and land birds in spring and fall.

Santa Ana NWR, Rt. 1, Alamo 78516. Year-round home of many Mexican species and birds found in south Texas, including Least Grebes, Plain Chachalacas, and Green Jays.

Utah

Bear River Migratory Bird Refuge, Box 459, Brigham City 84302. Migrant waterfowl stop in February, marsh birds in March, shorebirds in April; many of these water-loving birds stay to breed in May and June. Hundreds of thousands of waterfowl, mainly pintails and Green-winged Teal, pass through in fall. Tundra Swans gather here in mid-October.

Ouray NWR, Randlett. For information: 447 East Main, Vernal 84078. Resting place in spring and fall for waterfowl and endangered Whooping Cranes with their Sandhill Crane foster parents.

Vermont

Missisquoi NWR, Rt. 78, Swanton 05488. Inundated with migrating ducks in April and mid-September.

Virginia

Back Bay NWR, Sandpiper Road, Virginia Beach. For information: Pembroke Office Park, Building 2, Suite 218, Virginia Beach 23462. Migrant shorebirds and waterfowl in spring (March-April) and fall (October-December). Winter haven for waterfowl.

Chincoteague NWR, Box 62, Chincoteague 23336. Outstanding views of migrant ducks (February-March, October-December), shorebirds (April-May, mid-July-September), and wintering waterfowl, including a major portion of the population of Greater Snow Geese. Migrating water birds stop at nearby *Assateague Island* in May and from July to September.

Washington

Mount Rainier NP, Star Rt., Ashford 98304. From early June to mid-July western species nest amid spectacular wild flowers in habitats ranging from lowland forests (thrushes, wrens) to subalpine meadows (Blue Grouse, Water Pipits).

Olympic NP, 600 East Park Avenue, Port Angeles 98362. Birdlife ranges from curlews and cormorants at sea level to Blue Grouse and ravens in the high country.

Turnbull NWR, Rt. 3, Cheney 99004. Canada Geese begin nesting in April, ducks in May. Transient waterfowl mass in September and October. Pygmy Nuthatches and California Quail common all year.

West Virginia

Dolly Sods Wilderness and Scenic Area, Monongahela NF, Box 240, Petersburg 26847. Hawk and warbler migration peaks in September. One of the largest birdbanding stations on the east coast.

Wisconsin

Horicon NWR, Rt. 2, Mayville 53050. One of the world's largest gatherings of Canada Geese in March and April, late September to early November.

Necedah NWR, Star Rt. West, Necedah 54646. Thousands of Sandhill Cranes, as well as Canada Geese and other waterfowl, touch down in April, October, and early November.

Wyoming

Grand Teton NP, Box 170, Moose 83012. Nesting area for Canada Geese, Great Blue Herons, and sparrows from April to July. Trumpeter Swans breed here and at the nearby *National Elk Refuge* in April and May.

Yellowstone NP, Box 168, Yellowstone National Park 82190. Clark's Nutcrackers and Mountain Bluebirds common in summer, along with nesting waterfowl and water birds.

Canada

Alberta

Banff NP, Banff TOL OCO. Waterfowl and mountain species abundant from April through fall migration.

British Columbia

Kootenay NP, Box 220, Radium Hot Springs VOA 1MO. Pine Siskins, Gray Jays, American Dippers, owls, and other forest dwellers common year round.

Mount Revelstoke and Glacier NPs, Box 350, Revelstoke VOE 2SO. Look for warblers—some migrating, some breeding— from May to early July.

Pacific Rim NP, Box 280, Ucluelet VOR 3AO. Waterfowl and shorebirds arrive in spring, when resident eagles gather to feed on spawning herring.

Manitoba

Churchill. For information: Department of Natural Resources, Box 24, Winnipeg R3H OW9. Most accessible breeding locale in North America of high arctic species—Arctic Loons, Arctic Terns, Ross' Gulls, shorebirds, waterfowl, owls, and songbirds.

Oak Hammock Marsh Wildlife Management Area, near Winnipeg. For information: Department of Natural Resources, Box 24, Winnipeg R3H OW9. Spring and fall bring migrating hawks, shorebirds, waterfowl, and land birds. Ducks and other marsh birds nest in spring and summer.

New Brunswick

Grand Manan Island. For information: Canadian Wildlife Service, Box 1590, Sackville EOA 3CO. Seabirds, herons, shorebirds, and songbirds abundant from June through September. Songbird migration peaks in late May and from late August to early September.

Machias Seal Island. For information: Canadian Wildlife Service, Box 1590, Sackville EOA 3CO. Arctic and Common Terns, Razorbills, and Atlantic Puffins nest here from mid-May to mid-August. Visitors are encouraged to circle the island by boat rather than to land.

Newfoundland

C.N. Ferry from Port aux Basques, Newfoundland, to North Sydney, Nova Scotia. For information: San Marine Reservation Bureau, Box 520, Port aux Basques AOM 1CO. Rare opportunity to view seabirds seldom seen from land.

Cape St. Mary's Seabird Sanctuary, near Placentia. For information: Newfoundland Wildlife Division, Box 4750, Pleasantville, St. John's A1C 5T7. Second largest colony of Northern Gannets in North America. Kittiwakes, Razorbills, and world's southernmost colony of Thick-billed Murres nest here from April to August.

Gros Morne NP, Box 130, Rocky Harbour AOK 4NO. Late June and early July are the best times to see resident ptarmigan, as well as breeding gulls and terns. Shorebirds and waterfowl stop here in spring and fall.

Northwest Territories

Wood Buffalo NP, Box 750, Fort Smith XOE OPO. The northernmost colony of Whooping Cranes; white pelicans breed nearby. Fall gatherings of waterfowl.

Nova Scotia

Brier Island. For information: Nova Scotia Bird Society, 1747 Summer Street, Halifax B3H 3A6. Migrating shorebirds, warblers, and hawks in spring and fall. Island can be reached by ferry.

Cape Breton Highlands NP, Ingonish Beach BOC 1LO. Spring is best time to see Bald Eagles, seabirds, loons, gulls, cormorants, and warblers.

Ontario

Point Pelee NP, Rt. 1, Leamington N8H 3V4. Stopover for astonishing numbers of warblers and other songbirds in spring, especially mid-May, and hawks and Turkey Vultures in fall, especially mid-September.

Prince Edward Island

Prince Edward Island NP, Box 487, Charlottetown C1A 7L1. Prolific nesting area for Great Blue Herons. Water bird and shorebird migration from late July to early fall.

Quebec

Bonaventure Island. For information: Percé Wildlife Interpretation Center, Box 190, Percé GOC 2LO. One of the world's largest colonies of Northern Gannets. Thousands of Razorbills, Black Guillemots, Common Murres, and other seabirds also breed here. Island accessible only by boat.

Gaspesie PP, Box 550, Ste. Anne des Monts GOE 2GO. In spring look for migrating raptors and nesting songbirds, such as warblers and sparrows.

Saskatchewan

Cypress Hills PP, Box 850, Maple Creek SON 1NO. Raptors, herons, pelicans, cormorants, and songbirds nest here in spring and summer.

Prince Albert NP, Box 100, Waskesiu Lake SOJ 2YO. Breeding ground for water birds, waterfowl, woodpeckers, and other northern species.

Yukon Territory

Dempster Highway. For information: Yukon Conservation Society, Box 4163, Whitehorse Y1A 3T3. Ptarmigan live year round along this 451-mile road from the Klondike Highway to Inuvik, NWT. Arctic species, such as Surfbirds and Gyrfalcons, breed here in spring and summer.

Type composition by National Geographic's Photographic Services. Color separations by Beck Engraving Co., Inc., Philadelphia, Pa.; Chanticleer Co., Inc., New York, N.Y.; The Lanman Progressive Companies, Washington, D. C. Printed and bound by R. R. Donnelley & Sons Co., Chicago, Ill. Paper by S. D. Warren, Boston, Mass.

Library of Congress CIP Data

The Wonder of birds.

Bibliography: p.
Includes index.
1. Birds—Behavior. 2. Birds, Protection of.
I. National Geographic Book Service.
QL698.3.W66 1983 598.297 83-12141
ISBN 0-87044-470-0
ISBN 0-87044-471-9 (deluxe)